IDENTIFYING ANIMAL TRACKS

Mammals, Birds and Other Animals
of the Eastern United States

by
Richard Headstrom

DOVER PUBLICATIONS, INC., NEW YORK

Published in Canada by General Publishing Company, Ltd., 30 Lesmill
Road, Don Mills, Toronto, Ontario.
Published in the United Kingdom by Constable and Company, Ltd., 10
Orange Street, London WC2H 7EG.

This Dover edition, first published in 1983, is an unabridged and
unaltered republication of the work originally published by Ives Washburn,
Inc., New York, in 1971 under the title *Whose Track Is It?*

Manufactured in the United States of America
Dover Publications, Inc., 180 Varick Street, New York, N.Y. 10014

Library of Congress Cataloging in Publication Data

Headstrom, Richard, 1902–
    Identifying animal tracks.

    Reprint. Originally published: Whose track is it? New York : Washburn, c
1971.
    Includes index.
    1. Animal tracks—Atlantic States. 2. Animal tracks—United States. I.
Title.
QL768.H4   1983   591.5   82-17814
ISBN 0-486-24442-3

**To
My Wife**

Preface

In the *Bulletin* of the Massachusetts Audubon Society of January, 1950, I published an article called "Whose Track Is That? A Guide to Animal Tracks Found in Massachusetts," which was afterwards issued as a reprint. Several years later I published some material in *A Curriculum Guide for Intermediate Grade Teachers*, printed by the Massachusetts Department of Education, under the title of "Tracking Animals."

During the past twenty years this material and the reprint have been so extensively used by various groups interested in the outdoors and by the public at large, that it recently occurred to me that it might prove worthwhile to expand the material originally published by the Audubon Society to include the tracks of all the mammals found east of the Mississippi and to include also material on the tracks of other animals such as birds, frogs, toads, salamanders, snakes, lizards, turtles, and insects and other invertebrates.

Hence the present book, which does not presume to be the definitive work on animal tracks, but is merely a guide to help those of us who enjoy the outdoors to identify the tracks that we are apt to come across in the snow, in the mud of a streamside, in the sand of a pond shore and in that of the sea beach, and to learn how to read the stories they tell.

Contents

Illustrations

(*pages 85–138*)

Introduction

We may have the first snowfall in November or December, or even in October. Depending on where we live, we may not have more than a dusting before the new year. But I can remember as a boy going coasting on Thanksgiving.

We view the first snowstorm with mixed feelings. In a way we like to see the snow again but when we think of the hazards it creates in our modern way of life, we are not too sure. But it is always a problem to those wild animals that are active during the winter season, since food often becomes scarce or inaccessible. To be aware of this, you need only look out the window at your feeding station and watch the birds there. The birds, however, are not your only visitors. Though you may not see some of them you know these other visitors have been there because they leave their calling cards in the snow.

To many of us such calling cards might as well be blank, for unless we actually see these visitors we don't know who they are. But if we can read the cards, their identity is easily revealed.

To learn to identify the animals whose footprints we find in the snow is not very difficult, for every animal makes its own distinctive prints or series of prints in the form of a track pattern. You need only go out to the nearest field or patch of woods after a snowstorm and compare a few of the prints that you find in the smooth sheet of new snow to see that they are as different from each other and as distinctive as a series of signatures in a hotel register.

Not only do the prints help us identify the animals that made them, but the arrangement of the prints teaches us something of their habits. As you watch a gray squirrel cavort in your backyard, in the woods, or in a city park, you can imagine what sort of prints it will leave in the snow. You will find that prints of all four feet are made with each bound and that the prints of the two hind feet are paired; that is, they are side by side and in front of the prints made by the front feet. And what may seem strange is that the hind feet prints indicate the direction of travel; a fact that can easily be verified by looking at the toe marks.

All mammals that travel over the ground by bounding —mice, rats, squirrels, and rabbits—make the same kind of track pattern* though the position of the front feet prints may differ; that is, they may either be paired or one may be a little in advance of the other. Paired front feet prints are typical of the bounding animals that climb, such as the red and gray squirrels and the deer mouse. Alternate front footprints are mostly made by terrestrial mammals such as the rabbit and the meadow mouse.

One set of prints that is common everywhere is that of the domestic or house cat. A glance at the prints is enough to see that the animal walks on its toes, for only toe marks appear in its prints. The prints form a single line because the cat commonly puts a hind foot into the impression formed by a front foot. The dog and the fox

* The weasel and mink when galloping make a similar track pattern that is typical of the rodents.

also walk on their toes but the cat's prints are easily distinguished since a cat walks with its claws retracted and hence claw marks do not appear in its prints. At first glance the track of a dog may appear to be much like that of a fox but a careful comparison will show that the prints of the fox are more or less in a straight line and that the toe pads of the dog are somewhat larger, though in deep snow it is difficult to distinguish toe pad marks from claw marks.

Animals that walk on their toes are said to be digitigrade. These animals usually rely on speed to overtake their prey or to escape from their enemies. In addition to the three already mentioned, others that travel on their toes are the deer, moose, cow, goat, sheep, pig, and horse. All make fairly distinctive prints that are easy to identify once you get to know them.

Animals that have no need to hurry, either to capture their food or to elude their enemies, such as the porcupine with its quills and vegetarian diet and the skunk with its potent scent gland and omnivorous diet, are more elaborate in their movements and hence place both heels and toes to the ground. These animals are said to be plantigrade as also are the bear, raccoon, opossum, and woodchuck whose track is not often seen in the snow since it hibernates during the winter season. All of these animals make their own characteristic prints and track pattern though the track pattern may vary according to the gait. Thus the skunk's prints may sometimes form a diagonal line pattern.

In the track of some animals, the tail leaves a mark and thus becomes an important feature of the track pattern. In the track of the muskrat, for instance, the tail mark forms a strong curving line between the row of footprints. In that of the deer mouse it forms a straight continuous line between the rows of footprints as well as between the bounds unless they are of unusual length. When the cottontail sits, its tail makes a small round mark in the snow.

The sparrow, junco, goldfinch, and other winter birds also leave their prints in the snow. The size and shape of the prints, the number of toes and their arrangement serve to identify them and to provide us with a clue to their habits; for instance, whether a given bird hops or walks or does both. Other clues are marks such as those made by the fringe of hairs that grow out on the grouse's toes and that function as a kind of snowshoe to assist the bird in walking on top of the snow, or the semi-circles of separate marks made by the tips of wing feathers where they touch the snow when the bird takes to flight.

Learning to identify the prints of our wild creatures can be an interesting year-round pastime since tell-tale prints may also be found in mud and sand. On the muddy banks of a stream you can often see the characteristic prints of the raccoon and mink or those of a heron or a snipe, and along the sandy stretches of the sea beach the prints of hundreds of sandpipers as well as those of the gulls and terns can be seen. Here, too, you will find the bands of dots made by a crab or the winding trail left by a periwinkle or some other mollusk.

On a dusty country road, you may discover the prints of a toad, or the track of a snake, or the curious wide trail flanked with tiny footprints and with a short curving line here and there in the center that shows a turtle has passed that way dragging its tail behind. Or visit a sand dune where the prints of a grasshopper or a beetle stand out in bold relief. Indeed, every animal that moves over the surface of the ground leaves a track of some kind if the ground is soft enough to take an impression. Even the earthworm leaves its distinctive trail in the mud. Have you ever seen the track of a centipede or hundred-legs?

You do not have to go farther than your own backyard to find tracks, for throughout the year a large number of animals come and go there, day and night, and they all leave their calling cards.

Equally as interesting as learning how to identify the prints and tracks of various animals is learning how to read the stories they tell. Though this takes a little more patience and effort, the results are fascinating.

PART I

TRACKS

OF

MAMMALS

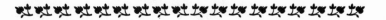

How to Use the Key

When identifying a track by means of the key on the following pages, the first factor to consider is the presence or absence of a tail mark. Assuming we have found a track in the snow in our yard, we note first of all that a tail mark is present. Starting with number 1, we find that we have a choice between "with a tail mark" and "without a tail mark." Since there is a tail mark in our hypothetical track we proceed to number 2, and here we have a choice between "prints paired" and "prints not paired." Examining our track, we find that the prints are paired, and so we go to number 3. We now learn that we must measure the front foot prints and on doing so find that they measure "less than 1 inch." This takes us to number 4 where we find that the front feet prints of two mammals measure ¼″ x ¼″. This means that we must now measure the prints of the hind feet. When we do so we find that they are ⅜″ x ½″. Hence we conclude that the prints were made by a deer mouse that must have ventured into our yard from the nearby woods, a normal habitat of the little rodent.

A word about the drawings and measurements (for taking measurements a tape measure should be used): The prints and tracks, as drawn, are purposely a more graphic delineation than those you will find in nature and

3

show much more detail than the actual prints, for only rarely are conditions in nature ideal for clear-cut impressions. The drawings are offered merely for a general check and not for specific identification—the key serves that end.

When using the key, allowances must be made for variation, especially in the measurements. However, the size of the prints are average. Many variations do occur; variations that are due to the age and sex of the animal and the nature of the medium in which the prints were made, such as shallow or deep snow, or mud or sand. Indeed, the same animal's prints made in mud might look quite different when made in snow. Prints, when freshly made, might appear different from those that have been exposed to the warm rays of the sun where they may have become enlarged or otherwise distorted. In many instances the gait of an animal influences the character of the track pattern, thus a walking track pattern may differ from a running track pattern.

The key and drawings should serve as a means of identifying the tracks described, unless they are completely distorted, in which case it would be impossible to identify them anyway. Sometimes a track may be found that doesn't seem to fit the key or the drawings simply because it is incomplete or not all there. Parts may be missing due to the irregularity of the ground or some other factor. A final note: When the identity of a track may be in doubt, a check of the habitat and range of the animal in question may resolve the problem. At times you may have to use a little ingenuity in determining the identity of a set of prints or track, but that is what adds interest to this outdoor pastime.

Key to Mammal Tracks

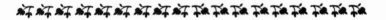

A. Footprints

1a.	With a tail mark	2[1]*
1b.	Without a tail mark	9
2a.	Prints paired, that is, more or less side by side	3
2b.	Prints not paired	6
3a.	Front foot prints less than 1 inch in length	4
3b.	Front foot prints more than 1 inch in length	5
4a.	FF $\frac{3}{16}''$ x $\frac{3}{16}''$, HF $\frac{3}{16}''$ x $\frac{3}{8}''$, running, $1\frac{3}{4}''$ leaps	**Common Shrew**[2]

Grassy fields, woodlands, swamps, meadows, and marshes.

Maine west to North Dakota south through Illinois, northern Kentucky, and in the east south to New Jersey and the mountains of North Carolina and Tennessee.

Smoky Shrew

Shady, damp woods.
New England west to eastern Ohio and south in mountains to northern Georgia.

* Refers to Notes.

5

Least Shrew

Dry fallow fields, marshy woods,
and meadows.
New York south to Florida and westward
to the Mississippi.

4b. FF ¼″ x ¼″, HF ½″ x ½″, running
2″ leaps   **Short-tailed Shrew**[3]
Weedy and dry upland fields, damp
woods, and marshes.
Eastern United States west to the Mississippi.

4c. FF ¼″ x ¼″, HF ⅜″ x ½″, running,
3″ leaps   **Deer Mouse**[4]
Grasslands, cornfields, woodlands, and
sand dunes of beaches.
New England south in the mountains to
Georgia and west to the Mississippi.

Old-field Mouse

Dry neglected sandy fields, rocky hill-
sides, uplands, beaches, and river bottoms.
Central and northern Alabama to central
Georgia and south to northern Florida.

White-footed Mouse

Woodlands, woodland borders, and
brushy areas.
New England south to central North Carolina, central South Carolina, central Georgia, central Alabama, and west to the
Mississippi.

Cotton Mouse

Low swamplands, wooded swamps,
and wet brushy areas.

Dismal Swamp region of Virginia south to
Florida, westward through Louisiana and
from the southern Smoky Mountains westward through Tennessee, Alabama, Mississippi, and north to southern Illinois.

Golden Mouse

Wooded and brushy areas, thickets of
honeysuckle and greenbrier, dense hemlock forests, woodland borders, low
ground, and swamp woodland.

From southeastern Virginia south to central Florida and west to southern Illinois
and Louisiana.

4d.   FF ¼" x ½", HF ½" x 1¼", slow, hopping,
      2½" leaps   **Jumping Mouse**[5]

Meadow Jumping Mouse

Dry fields and open meadows.

Canadian border south to North Carolina
and northwestern Oklahoma.

Woodland Jumping Mouse

Woodlands, sphagnum bogs, and
willow-alder swamps.

Maine west to Wisconsin and south in the
Appalachians to North Carolina.

4e.   FF ½" x ½", HF ½" x 1½", hopping,
      4" leaps   **Brown Rat**[6]

Grain fields, farmlands, waste places,
beaches, and salt marshes.

Throughout eastern United States west to
the Mississippi.

4f.   FF ½″ x ½″, HF ⅜″ x ⅝″, bounding,
      8″ to 12″ bounds   **Least Weasel**[7]
      Farming country and woodlands.
            Western Pennsylvania south into the
            mountains of North Carolina and west-
            ward through Ohio, northern Indiana to
            the Dakotas.

4g.   FF ¾″ x ½″, HF ⅝″ x 1″, bounding,
      12″ to 18″ leaps   **Long-tailed Weasel**[8]
      Fields, cutover brush lands, woodlands,
      thickets and wooded swamps.
            Throughout eastern United States west to
            the Mississippi.

5a.   FF 1½″ x 1½″, HF 1½″ x 1¾″, bounding,
      12″ to 23″ leaps   **Mink**[9]
      Diverse habitats but usually not far
      from water.
            Throughout eastern United States west to
            the Mississippi.

5b.   FF 2″ x 2″, HF 2½″ x 2¾″, bounding,
      20″ leaps   **River Otter**[10]
      In the vicinity of water, inland water-
      ways, estuaries, and about islands.
            Throughout eastern United States west to
            the Mississippi.

6a.   Four-toed   7[11]
6b.   Five-toed   8[11]

7a. FF ¼″ x ¼″, HF ³⁄₁₆″ x ¼″, walking,
     1″ stride   **Harvest Mouse**[12]
          Grassy fields, brushy borders, waste
          places, brackish meadows, and wet
          bottomlands.
               Virginia and Ohio south to Florida and
               Louisiana.

7b. FF 1¼″ x 1¼″, HF 1½″ x 3″, walking,
     8″ stride   **Muskrat**[13]
          Marshy ponds, marshes, and wooded
          swamps.
               New England south to central South Caro-
               lina, northern Georgia, central Alabama,
               and southern Mississippi.

8a. FF 1¾″ x 1½″, HF 1¼″ x 1¾″, walking,
     12″ stride   **Opossum**[14]
          Open woods, swamps, and waste lands.
               New England south to Florida and west
               from the Atlantic coast to the Mississippi.

8b. FF 2½″ x 3½″, HF 5½″ x 7″, walking,
     16″ stride   **Beaver**[15]
          Lakes, ponds, and slow-moving streams.
               Generally throughout eastern United States
               west to the Mississippi.

9a. Prints diagonal   10
9b. Prints paired, that is, more or less side by
     side   11
9c. Prints not paired   18
9d. Prints more or less in a straight line   25

10a.   FF 1½″ x 2″, HF 1½″ x 2½″, gallop,
        12″ leaps   **Striped Skunk**[16]
            Diverse habitats.
                Throughout eastern United States west to
                the Mississippi.

10b.   FF 2″ x 2″, HF 2″ x 1¾″, running,
        6″ leaps   **Badger**[17]
            Open prairie country and flat rolling
            farmlands.
                Northern and western Ohio westward
                through the greater part of Michigan,
                northern Indiana, northern Illinois, and
                most of Wisconsin.

11a.   Both sets paired   12
11b.   Only one set paired   15
12a.   Front foot prints less than 1 inch in length   13
12b.   Front foot prints more than 1 inch in length   14
13a.   FF ³⁄₁₆″ x ³⁄₁₆″, HF ³⁄₁₆″ x ⅜″, running,
        1¾″ leaps   **Common Shrew**[2]
            See 4a for habitat and range.

                                                  Smoky Shrew
            See 4a for habitat and range.

                                                  Least Shrew
            See 4a for habitat and range.

13b.   FF ¼″ x ¼″, HF ½″ x ½″, running,
        2″ leaps   **Short-tailed Shrew**[3]
            See 4b for habitat and range.

13c.   FF ¼″ x ¼″, HF ⅜″ x ½″, running,
        3″ leaps   **Deer Mouse**[4]
            See 4c for habitat and range.

Old-field Mouse
See 4c for habitat and range.

White-footed Mouse
See 4c for habitat and range.

Cotton Mouse
See 4c for habitat and range.

Golden Mouse
See 4c for habitat and range.

13d. FF ¼″ x ¼″, HF ¼″ x ⅜″, running,
    6¼″ to 7½″ leaps   **House Mouse**[18]
    Fields, waste places, orchards, and
    backyards.
        Throughout eastern United States west to
        the Mississippi.

13e. FF ½″ x ½″, HF ½″ x 1½″, hopping,
    4″ leaps   **Brown Rat**[6]
    See 4e for habitat and range.

13f. FF ½″ x ½″, HF ¾″ x 1¾″, bounding,
    11″ to 29″ leaps   **Flying Squirrel**[19]

Southern Flying Squirrel
    Deciduous woods.
        Eastern United States except northern
        New Hampshire, northern Vermont and
        Maine west to the Mississippi.

Northern Flying Squirrel

Coniferous woods, stands of yellow birch and hemlock, less often in woods of maple and beech.

Maine to eastern New York and south in the mountains to North Carolina and Tennessee.

13g.   FF ½″ x ¾″, HF 1″ x 1¾″, bounding, 8″ to 30″ leaps   **Red Squirrel**[20]

Forested areas and woodlands, preferably stands of mixed conifers and hardwoods.

New England south through Pennsylvania and in the mountains to Georgia and west through northern Illinois and Minnesota.

14a.   FF 1″ x 1¼″, HF 1″ x 1½″, bounding, 4″ to 14″ leaps   **Spotted Skunk**[21]

Open areas, farmlands, cultivated fields, and wastelands.

Southeastern United States from West Virginia south to southern Florida, west to the Mississippi.

14b.   FF 1″ x 1½″, HF 1¼″ x 2½″, bounding, 24″ to 36″ leaps   **Gray Squirrel**[22]

Woodlands and city parks.

Throughout eastern United States west to the Mississippi.

14c.   FF 1″ x 1¾″, HF 1½″ x 2¾″, bounding, leaps to 36″   **Fox Squirrel**[23]

Woods, woodland groves, open borders of swamps and thickets.

From the Atlantic Coast, from Maryland and Florida, and from western Pennsylvania, west to the Mississippi.

14d. FF 2½″ x 3″, HF 2½″ x 4″, running, leaps to 20″ **Raccoon**[24]
Woods, forested regions, swamps, and in the vicinity of streams.
Throughout eastern United States west to the Mississippi.

15a. Front foot prints less than 1 inch in length 16
15b. Front foot prints more than 1 inch in length 17
16a. FF ½″ x ⅜″, HF ¾″ x 1¼″, running, 6″ leaps **Chipmunk**[25]
Woods, woodland borders, and hedgerows.
New England south to central Georgia and west to the Mississippi.

Thirteen-lined Ground Squirrel
Fields and pastures.
Wisconsin, Illinois, Indiana, and Michigan eastward to central Ohio.

Franklin's Ground Squirrel
Fields, preferably with some hedges and bushy borders.
Northwestern Indiana, northern and central Illinois, north into central Wisconsin.

16b. FF ½″ x ½″, HF ½″ x ¾″, speeding, 9″ leaps **Meadow Mouse**[26]
Dry fields with a protecting cover of dead grass and herbs, low meadows, swampy pastures, beaches, and salt meadows.

Maine south to South Carolina and west to the Mississippi.

Red-backed Mouse

Cool, damp, shaded woods, meadows, sphagnum bogs.

New England south to northern New Jersey and in the mountains to North Carolina and Tennessee, westward through the northern part of lower Michigan Peninsula and much of northern Wisconsin.

Pine Mouse

Dry fields and woodlands.

Central New Hampshire south to Florida and west to the Mississippi.

16c. FF ½″ x ½″, HF ⅜″ x ⅝″, bounding, 8″ to 12″ bounds   **Least Weasel**[7]

See 4f for habitat and range.

16d. FF ½″ x ¾″, HF ⅝″ x 1⅞″, speeding, 7″ to 8″ leaps   **Wood Rat**[27]

Low, wet ground, swamps, and rocky cliffs of mountainsides, and in caves.

Southern Indiana and Illinois south to Georgia and west to the Mississippi, along the coast from South Carolina to central Florida and west to the Mississippi, from western Connecticut and the mountains of southern New York south through northern New Jersey, Pennsylvania, western Maryland, western Virginia to northern Alabama.

16e. FF ¾″ x ½″, HF ⅝″ x 1″, bounding, 12″ to 18″ leaps   **Long-tailed Weasel**[8]

See 4g for habitat and range.

17a. FF 1″ x 1″, HF 1¾″ x 3½″, speeding,
      leaps to 7′   **Cottontail**[28]

Eastern Cottontail
Farmlands, upland thickets, swampy
woods, woodland borders, and
shrubby areas.
   Throughout the eastern United States, except New England, east of the Mississippi.

New England Cottontail
Open woods, woodland borders, shrubby
areas, and thickets.
   Southern Maine, northern Vermont, and
   western New York south in Allegheny
   Mountains to southeastern Alabama.

17b. FF ¾″ x 1¼″, HF 1⅛″ x 1⅞″, bounding,
      9″ to 46″ leaps   **Marten**[29]
         Spruce and balsam forests.
            Northern Maine, northern New Hamp-
            shire, northern Vermont, and the Adiron-
            dacks.

17c. FF 1½″ x 1½″, HF 1½″ x 1¾″, bounding,
      12″ to 23″ leaps   **Mink**[9]
         See 5a for habitat and range.

17d. FF 2″ x 2″, HF 2½″ x 2¾″, bounding,
      20″ leaps   **River Otter**[10]
         See 5b for habitat and range.

17e. FF 3″ x 2½″, HF 3″ x 2½″, bounding,
      26″ leaps   **Fisher**[30]
         Spruce and balsam forests.
            Northern New England and the Adiron-
            dacks.

17f.   FF 3″ x 3″, HF 3½″ x 6½″, slow hop,
       leaps to 2′   **Varying Hare**[31]
           Forested areas, brushy semi-open tracts,
           cedar swamps, and wooded hillsides.
               Maine south to southern Massachusetts,
               west to eastern New York and south to the
               western Allegheny Mountains of West Vir-
               ginia and western Virginia.

17g.   FF 3″ x 4″, HF 4″ x 7″, galloping,
       leaps to 37″   **Black Bear**[32]
           Forested and mountain areas.
               Parts of Maine, northern New Hampshire
               and Vermont, western Massachusetts,
               much of New York and Pennsylvania,
               northern Michigan and Wisconsin, moun-
               tains of West Virginia and Virginia, and
               the Smoky Mountains of North Carolina
               and Tennessee.

18a.   Toe marks not showing or indistinct   19
18b.   Toe marks showing or distinct   20
19a.   FF ³⁄₁₆″ x ³⁄₁₆″, HF ³⁄₁₆″ x ⅜″, walking
                                          Common Shrew[2]
       See 4a for habitat and range.

                                          Smoky Shrew
       See 4a for habitat and range.

                                          Least Shrew
       See 4a for habitat and range.

19b.   FF ¼″ x ¼″, HF ½″ x ½″, walking
                                    Short-tailed Shrew[3]
       See 4b for habitat and range.

19c. FF ¾″ x 1¼″, HF 1⅛″ x 1⅞″, walking,
9″ stride **Marten**[29]
See 17b for habitat and range.

19d. FF 1⅛″ x 1⅛″, HF 1⅛″ x 1⅛″, walking,
6″ stride **Domestic Cat**[33]
galloping, 32″ leaps **Domestic Cat**
Fields, roadsides, city parks, and
backyards.
Throughout eastern United States west to
the Mississippi.

19e. FF 1½″ x 1½″, HF 1½″ x 1¾″, walking
Mink[9]
See 5a for habitat and range.

19f. FF 1½″ x 1⅞″, HF 1½″ x 1¾″, walking,
6″ to 16″ stride **Gray Fox**[34]
Brushy country, woodlands, swamps,
and hammocks.
Eastern United States west to the Mississippi.

19g. FF 1¾″ x 1⅞″, HF 1¾″ x 1⅞″, walking,
14″ stride **Bobcat**[35]
Forests, thickets, swamps, rocky terrain
and mountains.
Throughout eastern United States west to
the Mississippi except possibly parts of the
Midwest.

19h. FF 1¾″ x 2½″, HF 1½″ x 2¼″, walking,
14″ stride **Coyote**[36]
Open brushy areas and woodlands.

Northern Wisconsin, northern Michigan,
western Illinois and northern Indiana and
sporadically through eastern states from
Maine to Florida.

19i.   FF 1½″ x 2¾″, HF 2″ x 3½″, walking,
        stride less than 1′   **Porcupine**[37]
        Woodlands, preferably those containing
        conifers.
            Maine to Pennsylvania, westward through
            northern Michigan and Wisconsin.

19j.   FF 2″ x 2″, HF 2½″ x 2¾″, walking
                                                 River Otter[10]
        See 5b for habitat and range.

19k.   FF 2″ x 2½″, HF 1¾″ x 2″, running
                                                 Red Fox[38]
        Dry uplands, woodlands, forests, swamps,
        marshes and lowlands.
            Eastern United States from Maine to Wis-
            consin, south to northern Georgia and
            Mississippi, less common southward.

19l.   FF 2¾″ x 2½″, HF 2½″ x 2″, walking
                                                 Domestic Dog
        galloping, leaps to 38″   (**Foxhound**)
        Fields, roadsides, waste places, and
        city parks.
            Throughout eastern United States west to
            the Mississippi.

19m.   FF 3″ x 2½″, HF 3″ x 2½″, bounding,
        26″ leaps   **Fisher**[30]
        See 17e for habitat and range.

20a. Four-toed, no claw marks showing 21[11]
20b. Four-toed, claw marks showing 22
20c. Five-toed, no claw marks showing 23[11]
20d. Five-toed, claw marks showing 24
21a. FF ½″ x ½″, HF ½″ x 1½″, walking,
    3″ stride   **Brown Rat**[6]
    See 4e for habitat and range.

21b. FF ½″ x ¾″, ⅝″ x 1⅞″, walking,
    3″ stride   **Wood Rat**[27]
    See 16d for habitat and range.

21c. FF 1⅛″ x 1⅛″, HF 1⅛″ x 1⅛″, walking,
    6″ stride   **Domestic Cat**[33]
    See 19d for habitat and range.

21d. FF 1¾″ x 1⅞″, HF 1¾″ x 1⅞″, walking,
    14″ stride   **Bobcat**[35]
    See 19f for habitat and range.

22a. FF ¼″ x ¼″, HF ⅜″ x ½″, slow
    running   **Deer Mouse**[4]
    See 4c for habitat and range.

22b. FF ¼″ x ¼″, HF ¼″ x ⅜″, slow
    running   **House Mouse**[18]
    See 13d for habitat and range.

22c. FF ½″ x ½″, HF ½″ x ¾″, walking,
    1½″ stride   **Meadow Mouse**[26]
    See 16b for habitat and range.

Red-backed Mouse
    See 16b for habitat and range.

Pine Mouse
See 16b for habitat and range.

22d. FF ½″ x ½″, HF ¾″ x ⅞″, walking
                                        Rice Rat[40]
      Wet meadows, marshes, and tidal flats.
      Southern New Jersey south to Florida and
      west to the Mississippi and north to Illi-
      nois.

22e. FF ½″ x ¾″, HF ¾″ x 1″, walking,
      1¼″ stride   **Cotton Rat**[41]
      Overgrown grass fields, farmlands, and
      thickets.
      Southern Virginia south to southern
      Florida and west to the Mississippi.

22f. FF ¾″ x ½″, HF ⅝″ x 1″, walking
                                  Long-tailed Weasel[8]
      See 4g for habitat and range.

22g. FF ¾″ x 1″, HF 1″ x 1¼″, running,
      3¾″ to 6½″ leaps   **Prairie Dog**[42]
      The prairie dog has largely disappeared
      from the short-grass prairies and open
      plains it once inhabited and today may
      be found chiefly in the national parks
      and other refuges of the Midwest.

22h. FF ¾″ x 1¼″, HF 1⅛″ x 1⅞″, walking
                                        Marten[29]
      See 17b for habitat and range.

22i.   FF 1″ x 1½″, HF 1¼″ x 2½″, walking
                                       Gray Squirrel[22]
    See 14b for habitat and range.

22j.   FF 1⅜″ x 1¾″, HF 1½″ x 2⅛″, walking
                                         Armadillo[43]
    Dense shady cover such as brush,
    woodland, cactus and chaparral.
      Parts of Louisiana and parts of Florida.

22k.   FF 1¼″ x 1½″, HF 1¼″ x 1¾″, walking,
    stride 3½″   **Woodchuck**[44]
    Open fields, hillsides, and woodland
    borders.
      Canadian border south to southeastern
      Virginia, and northern Alabama west to
      the Mississippi.

22l.   FF 1½″ x 1½″, HF 1½″ x 1¾″,
    walking   **Mink**[9]
    running, 11″ leaps   **Mink**
    See 5a for habitat and range.

22m. FF 1½″ x 2¾″, HF 2″ x 3½″, walking,
    stride less than 1′   **Porcupine**[37]
    See 19h for habitat and range.

22n.   FF 1¾″ x 2½″, HF 1½″ x 2¼″,
    walking, 14″ stride   **Coyote**[36]
    running, 16″ leaps   **Coyote**
    See 19g for habitat and range.

22o.   FF 2¾″ x 2½″, HF 2½″ x 2″, walking,
    stride up to 10″   **Domestic Dog**[39]
    See 19j for habitat and range.

23a. FF 2″ x 2″, HF 2½″ x 2¾″, running,
      15″ to 22″ leaps   **River Otter**[10]
         See 5b for habitat and range.

23b. FF 3″ x 4″, HF 4″ x 7″, loping, 37″ stride
                                          Black Bear[32]
         See 17g for habitat and range.

24a. FF 1″ x 1¼″, HF 1″ x 1½″, walking,
      5″ stride   **Spotted Skunk**[21]
         See 14a for habitat and range.

24b. FF 1½″ x 2″, HF 1½″ x 2½″, walking,
      5″ stride   **Striped Skunk**[16]
         See 10a for habitat and range.

24c. FF 1¾″ x 1½″, HF 1¼″ x 1¾″, walking,
      7″ stride   **Opossum**[14]
         See 8a for habitat and range.

24d. FF 2″ x 2″, HF 2″ x 1¾″, walking,
      6″ to 12″ stride   **Badger**[17]
         See 10b for habitat and range.

24e. FF 2½″ x 3″, HF 2½″ x 4″, walking,
      7″ stride   **Raccoon**[24]
         See 14d for habitat and range.

24f. FF 3″ x 2½″, HF 3″ x 2½″, walking,
      13″ stride   **Fisher**[30]
         See 17e for habitat and range.

24g. FF 3″ x 4″, HF 4″ x 7″, walking,
      12″ stride   **Black Bear**[32]
         See 17g for habitat and range.

25a.　FF 1⅛″ x 1⅛″, HF 1⅛″ x 1⅛″

Domestic Cat[33]

　　　See 19d for habitat and range.

25b.　FF 1½″ x 1⅞″, HF 1½″ x 1¾″, walking,
　　　6″ to 16″ stride　　　　　　　**Gray Fox**[34]
　　　See 19e for habitat and range.

25c.　FF 1¾″ x 1⅞″, HF 1¾″ x 1⅞″, walking,
　　　14″ stride　　　　　　　　　　**Bobcat**[35]
　　　See 19f for habitat and range.

25d.　FF 2″ x 2½″, HF 1¾″ x 2″, walking,
　　　8″ to 18″ stride　　　　　　　**Red Fox**[38]
　　　See 19i for habitat and range.

B. Hoof Prints

1a.　FP 6″ x 5″, HP 6″ x 4½″, solid, walking,
　　　stride 25″　　　　　　　**Domestic Horse**[45]
　　　　Fields, pastures, and farmlands.
　　　　　Throughout eastern United States west to
　　　　　the Mississippi.

1b.　Divided　　　　　　　　　　　　　　　　2
2a.　Hind prints less than 3 inches in length　　3
2b.　Hind prints 3 inches in length　　　　　　4
2c.　Hind prints more than 3 inches in length　 5
3a.　HP 2½″, walking　　　　　**Domestic Sheep**[46]
　　　　Fields, pastures, and farmlands.
　　　　　Throughout eastern United States west to
　　　　　the Mississippi.

3b.   HP 2⅝", walking, stride about 15"
                                              Domestic Goat[47]
      Fields, pastures, and farmlands.
      Throughout eastern United States west to
      the Mississippi.

3c.   HP 2½" to 3", galloping, leaps 6'
                                              White-tailed Deer[48]
      Woodlands and wooded swamps.
      Throughout eastern United States west to
      the Mississippi.

4a.   HP 3", walking, stride 10" to 11"
                                              Domestic Pig[49]
      Fields, pastures, and farmlands.
      Throughout eastern United States west to
      the Mississippi.

5a.   HP 4", walking, stride 17" to 21"
                                              Domestic Cow[50]
      Fields, pastures, and farmlands.
      Throughout eastern United States west to
      the Mississippi.

5b.   HP 7", trotting, stride, 43"   **Moose**[51]
      Spruce forests, swamps, and aspen thickets
      bordering northern lakes and rivers.
      Northern Maine, northern New Hamp-
      shire and Vermont; upper Michigan Penin-
      sula.

Notes

1. Although tail marks usually show well in snow, they are usually absent in mud since animals that drag their tails usually do not do so in mud; however tail marks do sometimes show in this medium.
2. Several species of shrews, such as the Common or Masked Shrew, the Smoky Shrew, and the Least Shrew, may be found throughout the eastern part of the United States. Their prints and track patterns are similar. The track of the shrew, which is usually seen in snow and rarely in mud or sand, resembles that of the Deer Mouse (see note 4 below) though it is somewhat smaller and perhaps shorter, its width or straddle being about an inch and sometimes as much as an inch and a quarter. The shrew has five toes on its front feet (which sometimes do not show up too well in snow) whereas the mouse has only four. Though often absent the curious grooved tail-mark is a distinctive feature of the track when the animal is hopping or walking.
3. The prints and tracks of the Short-tailed Shrew are similar to those of the Common Shrew but somewhat larger (see note 2 above).
4. There is said to be more than 15 species and over 75 subspecies of the genus Peromyscus occurring

north of Mexico to which the generic name of deer mouse has been given. Because of their white feet the deer mice are also known as the white-footed mice; various species have been given such names as the Old-field Mouse or Beach Mouse, the White-footed or Woodland Mouse, the Cotton Mouse, and the Golden Mouse. The prints and track pattern (the four-print pattern) are all similar though individual prints vary slightly in size. The track of the deer mouse may sometimes be mistaken for that of the house mouse (see note 18 below) though the track of the house mouse does not show a tail mark. It also resembles the track of the shrew (see note 2 above) though it is much larger, being from 1½ to 1¾ inches in width, and having front prints showing only four toes. The shrew shows five toes although in snow the toes of either animal are not always easily distinguished from each other.

5. Since both the meadow jumping mouse and the woodland jumping mouse hibernate, their prints and tracks are not likely to be seen in snow; as a matter of fact both live in grassy and brushy areas and their tracks are not often seen at all though sometimes they may be found in mud. The prints and tracks of both species are similar although those of the woodland species may be slightly larger. The leaps are usually not much more than a foot or two yet leaps of from 6 to 12 feet or more have been recorded.

6. The track of the brown or Norway rat is distinguished by the small four-fingered, handlike print of the front foot and the long heel impression of the hind foot. The track of the black rat, a species common in the South, is similar to that of the brown rat. The straddle is about 3 inches.

7. Except for a difference in the size of the prints and in the width of the track, which is from 1¼ to 1⅝ inches, the prints and track of the least weasel are similar to those of the long-tailed weasel (see note 8 below).

8. When running, the weasel's hind feet are usually placed, either nearly or completely, in the prints formed by the front feet so that the track appears to be a series of twin prints, placed slightly ahead of one another. However, sometimes the prints of the front feet may show behind the prints of the hind feet. Quite often one leap may be short and the next long so that the track may show alternating short and long leaps. The toes rarely show. Only under unusual conditions may the imprint of the toes be seen. The width of the track pattern may be as much as 3 inches. Though variations frequently occur, the track follows a fairly general pattern and once it becomes familiar it may easily be recognized thereafter. A tail mark may or may not be present.

9. The track of the mink is usually in the familiar double-print pattern—a larger version of the weasel's—and is made by the hind feet being placed in (or almost in) the prints made by the front feet. However, there are a number of variations in the mink track. Although the mink has five toes, only four register in the print. The width of the track pattern may be from 2¼ inches in mud to 3½ inches in snow.

10. The track of the otter is much like that of the mink but on a larger scale. The inner toe of the hind print often appears prominently out to one side, and though the web does not leave a noticeable mark on a firm surface it usually leaves an imprint in mud. The prints are rounded and the four blunt toes on all feet register

plainly, except in snow. The fifth toe registers less plainly than the other four blunt toes. In bounding, the hind prints are side by side and may cover the front prints. In running the hind prints are staggered ahead of the front prints.

11. Refers to front feet.

12. Clear cut prints of the harvest mouse are somewhat difficult to find since the animal usually stays in grassy, leafy, and brushy areas that do not take imprints too well.

13. The track of the muskrat is usually found near water. There is an appreciable difference in the size of the front footprint and the hind footprint. The front footprint often precedes the hind footprint in the track pattern but sometimes the hind footprint is foremost or may cover the front footprint. The inner toe of the front foot is so small that it usually doesn't leave an impression. The drag of the knife-like tail which shows clearly in mud is a distinctive feature of the track. The straddle is about 3½ inches.

14. The telltale mark of the opossum track is the large opposable big toe of the hind foot which has no nail or claw. A common walking track pattern shows the front and hind prints side by side but sometimes the hind footprint may be a little behind the front footprint. The tail may leave a sinuous drag mark or short alternating marks on both sides. The straddle is about 1¾ inches.

15. The beaver track is readily recognized because of the webbed hind foot and the absence of a claw mark on the second inside toe. An impression of the five toes of the front feet is not always in evidence; usually the front feet prints appear to be three- or four-toed.

Beaver tracks usually occur in the vicinity of ponds and streams.

16. The claws of the front feet are well developed and always show in the track of the striped skunk but the hind feet prints seldom show any claw marks. Its most characteristic track is the diagonal arrangement of the prints when galloping. In snow country, the skunk will curl up in its den during severe weather but a rise in temperature will lure it out even when the snow blanket is deep.

17. The track of the badger is extremely toed-in. The claws of the hind feet rarely leave an imprint. When running the animal makes a peculiar diagonal track; the hind feet being placed in front of the front feet. The width of the track is from 4 to 7 inches.

18. The track of the house mouse is rather like that of the deer mouse though its prints are not always paired. As this species usually lives in buildings its track is not often seen in the woods.

19. Since the flying squirrel is largely an arboreal animal and its movements are generally from tree to tree, its tracks on the ground are rather sketchy. The front feet prints are usually parallel but sometimes one front footprint is slightly ahead of the other. A "sitzmark" or landing spot is frequently a feature of the track. The straddle is 3¼ inches.

20. Since the red squirrel is more or less an arboreal animal and its home range is rather limited, its tracks are usually to be found within the narrow area of a small group of trees and appear to be going from tree to tree with one track often crossing another. Sometimes a track pattern will show one front footprint ahead of the other instead of being paired. The straddle is 3 to 4½ inches.

21. During severe winter weather the spotted skunk usually remains within its snug nest but on warm days will venture abroad. Then its tracks can be seen in the snow. Its track is smaller and shows quite a different pattern from that of the larger striped skunk. In walking its track shows an irregular pattern, while in bounding its track looks like that of a stubby-toed squirrel though the front footprints show five toes while the squirrel shows four.

22. The prints and track pattern of the gray squirrel when bounding are similar to those of the red squirrel but somewhat larger (see note 20 above). When walking the prints are alternate and not paired. The front footprints and the hind footprints are close together. The friction pads of the squirrel's feet often leave very distinct indentations. The straddle is from 4½ to almost 5 inches.

23. The prints and track pattern of the fox squirrel are like those of the gray squirrel but are slightly larger (see note 22 above). When bounding its front feet prints are paired behind the hind feet prints. When foraging the prints are not paired but the prints of the front and hind feet are close together.

24. The track of the raccoon is easy to identify because the hind feet rest flat on the ground and the prints look like those of a small child. The track pattern is suggestive of the black bear's in miniature. When walking the print of the left hind foot appears beside that of the right front foot.

25. Since the chipmunk hibernates during the winter in snow country, its tracks will be seen in snow only in fall and in early spring. Sometimes the prints of the front feet are parallel but usually one print is behind the other with both the hind footprints in front of

the front footprints. The individual prints of the chipmunk are much like those of the squirrel except for size. The prints and tracks of the ground squirrels are similar to those of the chipmunk and tree squirrels but the claws of the ground squirrels are larger and straighter than those of the tree squirrels, a difference which, however, may not be apparent in the track. The front footprints of the ground squirrels are one behind the other as in those of the chipmunk and are not paired as in those of the tree squirrels. Also, like the chipmunk, the ground squirrels go into hibernation except in the more southern parts of the country and hence their tracks are usually not seen in snow except in the early snowfalls of autumn and early spring.

26. The track of the meadow mouse, also known as the meadow vole and field mouse, when running is a double-print pattern similar to that of the weasel but on a much smaller scale. The meadow mouse, however, makes a variety of track patterns depending on the depth of the snow and the nature of the surface on which it is running, such as mud, sand, etc. The pattern is varied as well by its gait and speed. For all practical purposes there is little apparent difference between the tracks of the meadow mouse, the pine mouse, and the red-backed mouse.

27. The track of the wood rat is similar to that of the brown rat though its prints are slightly larger. Sometimes the front feet prints are paired.

28. Probably few tracks are as familiar as those of the cottontail which may often be seen in the outskirts of a city. The details of the rabbit's prints are usually blurred by the hair between the toes, which is especially long in winter. There are two species of cotton-

tails in the eastern half of the United States, the Eastern cottontail and the New England cottontail but the prints and tracks of both are alike.

29. The prints and track of the marten may be confused with those of the larger fisher and the somewhat smaller mink. These three species, together with the weasel, have similar track patterns and the only essential difference is that of size. The partly furred marten's front feet leave a less distinct and much more elongated imprint than that of a mink. When bounding the hind feet are placed either in the prints of the front feet or ahead of them. (If placed in front prints, the imprints on one side are slightly ahead of those on the other.) The straddle is from 2½ to 6 inches.

30. The size of the prints and length of the stride of the fisher are quite variable depending on the nature of the surface and the gait of the animal. In mud or sand the prints are somewhat smaller than they are in snow. See note 29 on marten above.

31. The track pattern of the varying hare, also known as the snowshoe rabbit, is similar to that of the cottontail but the prints are much larger. The toes of the hind feet spread to form a broad "snowshoe" effect on the surface of the snow. When not in a hurry the varying hare pairs the hind feet ahead of the front feet which also are almost paired, but when speeding it stretches both hind and front feet out diagonally.

32. In the typical walking gait the hind footprint appears a little ahead of the front footprint on the same side. The "big toe" of the bear's foot is the outer one and not the inner one as in the human foot. In shallow mud the little inside toe often does not leave a mark (or it leaves a faint one) so that the bear's print

appears to be four-toed. When galloping, with a leap of as much as 37 inches, the hind footprints appear before the front footprints. Sometimes the claws do not register. Since the black bear hibernates its track is not seen often in snow.

33. Though there is a variety of breeds of the domestic cat, its tracks are similar and the prints are much the same in size. The prints are smaller than those of the bobcat (see note 35 below) and are much rounder than those of the fox or small dog (see notes below). The absence of claw marks distinguishes the print of the cat from that of the dog or fox.

34. The prints of the gray fox are similar to those of the red fox (see note 38 below).

35. The track of the bobcat is similar to that of the domestic cat (see note 33 above) though the prints are somewhat larger. Like the prints of the cat, those of the bobcat show no claw marks. When running the length of its leaps vary considerably and may be from less than 4 to more than 8 feet depending on its need for speed.

36. The track of the coyote is usually like that of the dog (see note 39 below). As in the other Canidae, the front foot is larger than the hind foot.

37. The track of the porcupine is distinctive in its short waddling gait and its tendency to toe in. The animal is so short-legged that if the snow is very deep it plows a furrow with its body as it walks. The marks of the long claws are fairly well ahead of the footprints which usually show a pebbled design. Sometimes the hind footprints are ahead of the front footprints although at other times the front footprints are ahead. In snow the hind footprint usually registers in the front footprint. There are often drag marks of

the feet, sometimes connecting one print with the next. The straddle is 8 to 9 inches.

38. The track pattern of the red fox is traditionally that of a straight line but may vary with gait and speed. In the walking track the width of the track is about 3½ inches. One feature of the red fox pattern is the wide, sprawling front footprint as contrasted with the narrower, more pointed hind footprint. In shallow firm snow the prints may show only a portion of the toes and heel pad in which the heel pad seems to lie far behind the toes with the lobe not extending up between the two hind toes. In deeper snow and in soft mud the entire pad leaves an imprint. Straddle of the walking gait is about 3½ inches; of running gait about 4 inches.

39. There is a great variety of breeds and sizes of dogs but the prints and tracks of all of them are quite similar except for size. Usually the heel pads of the front feet make a clear imprint whereas the heel pads of the hind feet do not, either leaving out or showing only faintly the lateral lobes. Hence the heel pad of the hind foot tends to make a roundish or oval depression. Although the dog has five toes, only four leave an imprint. The front feet are wider than the hind feet.

40. Except for a slight difference in size the prints and tracks of both the rice rat and cotton rat are similar to those of the brown rat. See note 6 above.

41. See note 40 above.

42. There are two species of prairie dog, the black-tailed and the white-tailed, whose prints and tracks are similar.

43. Occasionally the reticulated imprint of the shell becomes part of the armadillo's track.

44. Since the woodchuck hibernates its track is not likely

to be seen in snow. In the walking gait the print of the hind foot is apt to be superimposed on that of the front foot. At times the hind footprint may be mistaken for that of the raccoon. However, the front footprint of the raccoon shows five toes, that of the woodchuck four toes.

45. The print of the horse can hardly be confused with the print of any other animal. Typically it shows the single round or oval hoof with the V mark of the frog in the middle. The print of the front hoof is wider and rounder than the print of the hind hoof. The prints of the mule are smaller and narrower.

46. The prints of the sheep may be confused with those of the deer and goat but may be distinguished from either by the blunt or less pointed head.

47. Prints with points in, outer margins heaviest.

48. When galloping, the white-tailed deer swings its hind feet far ahead of the front feet forming the familiar hind-footprints-in-front-of-the-front-footprints pattern so common in the track of the deer mouse and rabbit. Individual prints vary according to age. The prints of the doe are smaller and slimmer than those of the buck and point straight forward or inward while those of the buck point outward. The print of a full grown buck measures about 3 inches, that of the doe about 2½ inches.

49. The prints commonly show secondary toes or dew claws. The prints generally spread.

50. The prints of the cow are pointed and those of the front wider than those of the hind feet. Hind feet may be placed ahead, beside, or behind the prints made by the front feet.

51. The prints of the moose have points that curve inward and almost meet.

PART II

TRACKS

OF

BIRDS

Prints and Tracks of Birds

Although bird prints are sometimes quite distinctive, they lack, in general, the individuality of mammal prints. The print of the crow can usually be recognized by its rather large size, long hind toe, and the unequal spreading of the front toes. The print of the heron can be recognized because of its large size and widely spread toes. Webbed prints and the extreme tendency to toe-in are characteristics of the track pattern of the duck. All duck prints are much alike except for a slight difference in size so that it is difficult to identify the print of any one species with the possible exception of the wood duck whose print shows claw marks.

Perching birds, those, such as the sparrows, that spend most of their time in trees usually keep their feet together when on the ground and hop instead of walk so that their prints appear paired. Game birds, such as the quail and pheasant, as well as those that spend much of their time on the ground, like the robin and starling, walk or run so that their track pattern consists of a series of alternate prints. There are some exceptions such as the junco that both hops and walks; hence its track pattern consists of both paired and alternate prints.

To use the key to bird prints the procedure is the same as described in the key to mammal prints. Not all birds

that leave their autographs in mud or snow have been
included, only representative species and those most likely
to be encountered. Few people are apt to come upon the
prints and tracks of the loon or pied-billed grebe and yet
they are quite distinctive and typical of the water birds.

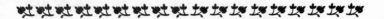

Key to Bird Tracks

1a.	Prints with front toes fully webbed	2
1b.	Prints with front toes partially webbed	8*
1c.	Prints with front toes lobate	11
1d.	Prints with front toes not webbed	12
2a.	Prints with 3 webbed toes, the fourth or hind toe not showing an imprint	3
2b.	Prints with 3 webbed toes, the fourth or hind toe showing only a slight imprint	4
2c.	Prints with 3 webbed toes, the fourth or hind toe showing an imprint	6
2d.	Prints with 4 webbed toes	7
3a.	Prints with the 3 front toes about the same length	**Common Loon**[1][†]

>Shores and marshes of inland lakes.
>Summer range: Canadian border south to northern Indiana, northern New York and New Hampshire. Winter range: mainly on salt water along the coast.

---

* Included in the key are those birds with partially webbed toes whose webs are likely to show in the prints; there are other birds, such as the herons, with slightly webbed toes though the webs are not always distinguishable in the print.

† Refers to Notes.

3b.   Prints with the middle front toe longer than
      the other two front toes   **Black-necked Stilt**[2]
      Wet meadows, ponds, streams, and sea
      beaches.
           Summer range: Florida, coastal South
           Carolina, and Louisiana. Winter range:
           Louisiana southward.

4a.   Prints 1″ in length   **Common Tern**[3]
      Sandy beaches and small islands.
           Summer range: locally from Canadian
           border south to Gulf of Mexico. Winter
           range: Florida southwards.

4b.   Prints 3″ in length   5
4c.   Prints 3½″ in length   **Herring Gull**[4]
      Beaches along the Atlantic Coast and
      shores of inland lakes.
           Summer range: Maine to Long Island and
           larger lakes of Canadian border. Winter
           range: Canadian border to Gulf of
           Mexico.

5a.   Prints showing claw marks   **Wood Duck**[5]
      Wooded swamps, river timber, apple
      orchards, and farmlands.
           Summer range: Gulf of Mexico north
           throughout the United States east of the
           Mississippi. Winter range: North to south-
           ern Illinois and Virginia.

5b.   Prints not showing claw marks   **Mallard**[6]
      Marshes, fields, and pastures.
           Summer range: Canadian border south to
           southeastern Illinois, southwestern In-

diana, and southern Ohio. Winter range:
Great Lakes and southern New England
south to Gulf of Mexico.

6a. Prints toed-in in track pattern **Canada Goose**[7]
Marshes and sloughs.
> Winter range: Canadian border south to
> Gulf of Mexico.

6b. Prints not toed-in in track pattern **Flamingo**[8]
Mud flats.
> Florida coast.

7a. Prints 4″ in length **Double-crested Cormorant**[9]
Coastal islands, small islands and rocky
reefs of inland lakes, and wooded swamps
in the interior.
> Summer range: locally throughout eastern
> United States west to the Mississippi,
> south to Florida and Gulf of Mexico. Win-
> ter range: along southern coasts.

7b. Prints 5″ in length **(Eastern) Brown Pelican**[10]
Islands in lakes and lagoons.
> Summer range: along Atlantic and Gulf
> Coasts from North Carolina to Louisiana.
> Winter range: Florida and Gulf Coast.

8a. Prints less than 1″ in length
Semi-palmated Sandpiper[11]
Sea beaches, sand-flats, and mud-flats.
> Winter range: along coast north to South
> Carolina.

8b. Prints between 1″ and 2″ in length   9
8c. Prints more than 2″ in length   10

9a.   Prints 1″ in length   **Semi-palmated Plover**[13]
      Sea beaches and salt marshes.
          Winter range: from South Carolina and
          Louisiana southwards.

9b.   Prints 1¼″ in length   **Spotted Sandpiper**[13]
      Margins of ponds and shores of streams.
          Summer range: throughout eastern United
          States south to northern South Carolina,
          Alabama, and southern Louisiana. Winter
          range: South Carolina and Louisiana
          southwards.

9c.   Prints 1⅜″ in length   **Wilson's Phalarope**[14]
      Wet or moist meadows, sloughs, grassy
      marshes, and marshy islands.
          Summer range: Canadian border south to
          northwestern Indiana.

10a. Prints with outer toe closer to the middle toe
      than the inner toe   **Greater Yellow-legs**[15]
      Mudflats, estuaries and pools in the marsh
      and along the shores of ponds and streams.
          Winter range: along the Atlantic and Gulf
          Coasts north to the Carolinas.

10b. Prints with outer toe not closer to the middle
      toe than the inner toe   **Willet**[16]
      Coastal marshes and inland prairies.
          Summer range: along the Atlantic Coast
          from Delaware Bay to Louisiana. Winter
          range: along Atlantic and Gulf Coasts
          from North Carolina to Louisiana.

11a. Prints 3″ in length **Pied-billed Grebe**[17]
Sloughs, marshy ponds, and lakes.
Summer range: Gulf States north through-
out eastern United States. Winter range:
north to Middle States and rarely to New
York and Ohio.

11b. Prints 4″ in length **Coot**[18]
Borders of sloughs and marshy ponds.
Summer range: Canadian border south to
Arkansas, Tennessee, and New Jersey;
casually to Florida. Winter range: Gulf of
Mexico north to Great Lakes and Long
Island.

12a. Prints with 3 front toes only 13
12b. Prints with 3 front toes and 1 hind toe 14
12c. Prints with 2 front toes and 2 hind toes **Flicker**[19]
Open country, lightly wooded regions,
deciduous woodlands, and orchards.
Summer range: throughout the United
States east of the Mississippi. Winter
range: north to the Great Lakes and southern New England.

13a. Prints ¾″ in length **Piping Plover**[20]
Sandy beaches.
Summer range: along the Atlantic Coast
from Maine south to North Carolina and
locally inland to Pennsylvania, northern
Ohio, and northeastern Illinois. Winter
range: along the coast from South Carolina to Louisiana.

13b. Prints ⅞" in length   **Sanderling**[21]
      Sea beaches.
      Winter range: along the Atlantic Coast
      from New Jersey southwards.

14a. Prints between 1" and 2" in length   15
14b. Prints between 2" and 3" in length   22
14c. Prints between 3" and 4" in length   27
14d. Prints more than 4" in length   29
15a. Prints 1⅛" in length   **English Sparrow**[22]
      Cities, towns, villages, and farms.
         Summer and winter ranges: throughout
         eastern United States west to the Mis-
         sissippi.

15b. Prints 1⅜" in length   **Killdeer**[23]
      Open situations.
         Summer range: Florida and Gulf of
         Mexico north to Canadian border. Winter
         range: Florida and Gulf of Mexico north
         to southern Illinois and southern New
         York.

15c. Prints 1½" in length   16
15d. Prints 1¾" in length   19
16a. Prints with hind toe in line with outer toe
                                                    Woodcock[24]
      Alder runs, swampy thickets, and along
      edges of woods.
         Summer range: northern Florida and
         southern Louisiana north throughout east-
         ern United States. Winter range: northern
         Florida and southern Louisiana north to
         New Jersey and Ohio Valley.

16b. Prints with hind toe not in line with outer toe   17
17a. Prints with outer toe same length as middle
      toe   **Bobwhite**[25]
      Fields and farming country.
         Summer and winter ranges: Gulf of
         Mexico north throughout eastern United
         States except northern Minnesota and
         northern Maine.

17b. Prints with outer toes not the same length
      as middle toe   18
18a. Prints paired, that is, side by side
                         Slate-colored Junco[26]
      Coniferous forests and deciduous wood-
      lands.
         Summer range: northern Minnesota, north-
         ern Michigan, Maine, and, in the higher
         Appalachians, to northern Georgia. Winter
         range: Canadian border south to Gulf of
         Mexico.

18b. Prints not paired   **Horned Lark**[27]
      Short grass fields.
         Summer range: Canadian border south to
         Ohio, West Virginia, and North Carolina.
         Winter range: Canadian border south to
         Gulf Coast, Georgia and (rarely) to
         Florida.

19a. Prints with hind toe in line with outer toe
                            Wilson's Snipe[28]
      Marshes and low ground.
         Summer range: Canadian border south to
         northwestern Pennsylvania and northern
         Illinois. Winter range: Gulf Coast north
         sparely.

19b.   Prints with hind toe not in line with outer toe   20
20a.   Prints of track more or less in a straight line
                                              Mourning Dove[29]

    Open country.
        Summer range: eastern United States east
        of the Mississippi except northern Maine.
        Winter range: Massachusetts and southern
        Michigan southward.

20b.   Prints of track not in a straight line   21
21a.   Prints with hind toe not showing too well
                                              Ruffed Grouse[30]

    Thick woods and wooded hills.
        Summer and winter ranges: eastern United
        States south to New Jersey and, in the
        Appalachians, to Georgia and Alabama
        and south in the Mississippi Valley to
        Michigan, Wisconsin and locally to Ohio
        and Indiana.

21a.   Prints with hind toe showing well   **Robin**[31]
        Woodlands, orchards and in the vicinity
        of human habitations.
            Summer range: throughout eastern United
            States south to western South Carolina,
            northern Georgia, and northern Louisiana.
            Winter range: southern United States
            north to Ohio Valley and the New Eng-
            land coast.

22a.   Prints 2″ in length   23
22b.   Prints 2¼″ in length   24
22c.   Prints 2½″ in length   25

22d. Prints 2⅞″ in length **Virginia Rail**[32]
Freshwater marshes.
> Summer range: eastern United States
> south to Kentucky and eastern North
> Carolina. Winter range: Gulf of Mexico
> north to North Carolina.

23a. Prints with claw marks showing
Eastern Meadowlark[33]
Grassy fields, grasslands, and pastures.
> Summer range: throughout eastern United
> States from eastern Minnesota south to
> Florida and Gulf of Mexico. Winter range:
> southern United States.

23b. Prints with no claw marks showing
Domestic Pigeon[34]
Cities, towns, and villages.
> Summer and winter ranges: throughout
> the United States east of the Mississippi.

24a. Prints with toes in an x-shaped arrangement
Burrowing Owl[35]
Prairies.
> Summer and winter ranges: central and
> southern Florida.

24b. Prints with toes not in an x-shaped
arrangement **Prairie Chicken**[36]
Open prairie country or bushy grasslands.
> Summer and winter ranges: Canadian bor-
> der south to southern Illinois, western
> Indiana, and northwestern Ohio.

25a.   Prints with toes in an x-shaped arrangement
                                Great Horned Owl[37]
        Heavily forested regions and scattered
        woodlands.
            Summer and winter ranges: throughout
            the United States east of the Mississippi.

25b.   Prints with toes not in an x-shaped
        arrangement   26
26a.   Prints alternate in track pattern   **Starling**[38]
        Rural and farming districts, cities and
        towns.
            Summer and winter ranges: throughout
            the United States east of the Mississippi.

26b.   Prints both alternate and paired in track
        pattern   **Wood Thrush**[39]
        Low, cool, damp forests, often near
        streams; sometimes in the vicinity of
        human habitations.
            Summer range: central Minnesota, central
            Wisconsin, New York, and central New
            England south almost to the Gulf of
            Mexico. Winter range: Florida south-
            wards.

27a.   Prints 3″ in length   ˏ   28
27b.   Prints 3½″ in length   **Ring-necked Pheasant**[40]
        Grassy fields and grainfields.
            Summer and winter ranges: mainly north
            of the Mason-Dixon line (Delaware,
            northern Maryland, southern Ohio, south-
            ern Indiana) to southern Maine, northern
            New York, southern Michigan, and Minne-
            sota.

27c.   Prints 3¾″ in length   **Sandhill Crane**[41]
     Marshes and wet prairies.
> Summer range: Minnesota, Michigan, and Wisconsin; also in Florida and southern Georgia. Winter range: Louisiana southwards.

28a.   Prints with inner and middle toes close
     together   **Crow**[42]
     Woodlands and coniferous forests, also grainfields, grassy fields, and pastures.
> Summer and winter ranges: throughout the United States east of the Mississippi.

28b.   Prints with inner and middle toes not
     close together   **(Eastern) Green Heron**[43]
     Wet woodlands and wooded areas along a pond or stream; occasionally dry woods and orchards.
> Summer range: throughout the United States east of the Mississippi. Winter range: Florida southwards.

29a.   Prints 4″ in length   30
29b.   Prints 5″ in length   32
29c.   Prints more than 5″ in length
     Great Blue Heron[44]
     Wooded swamps.
> Summer range: Florida Keys and the Gulf Coast north throughout the United States east of the Mississippi. Winter range: southern United States north rarely to Great Lakes and southern New England.

30a.   Prints with thick or stout toes
                                        Domestic Chicken[45]
        Farmlands and rural country.
            Summer and winter ranges: throughout
            the United States east of the Mississippi.

30b.   Prints with slender toes   31
31a.   Prints with hind toe almost equal in length
        to middle toe   **Florida Gallinule**[46]
        Freshwater marshes.
            Summer range: Gulf of Mexico north to
            Vermont, New York, and Minnesota. Win-
            ter range: north to South Carolina.

31b.   Prints with hind toe not equal in length to
        middle toe   **Black-crowned Night Heron**[47]
        Wooded swamps but sometimes dry hill-
        side thickets.
            Summer range: Florida and Gulf of
            Mexico north throughout the United States
            east of the Mississippi. Winter range:
            north to southern New England, southern
            New York, and Ohio.

32a.   Prints with middle toe slightly curved in   **Turkey**[48]
        Woodlands.
            Summer and winter ranges: north to
            Pennsylvania and eastern Kentucky.

32b.   Prints with middle toe not curved in
                                        American Bittern[49]
        Cattail marshes and meadows.
            Summer range: Gulf of Mexico north
            throughout the United States east of the
            Mississippi. Winter range: north to south-
            ern Illinois and Virginia.

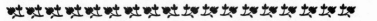

Notes

1. The loon is essentially an aquatic bird and is not often found on land, except at nesting time when its prints may be seen in the mud and sand of lake–shores. Because of the position of its legs, far back on its body, the loon finds it difficult to walk on land. The track pattern consists more or less of a series of halting prints.
2. The stilt with its long legs is a wading bird and its prints may often be seen in the sand and mud of sea beaches and the shores of ponds and streams. There is less of a web between the outer and middle toes than between the inner and middle toes.
3. The three-toed webbed track of the common tern may often be seen on sea beaches or on the shore of an island, or in an inland lake as a shallow imprint in the soft mud or sand. The length of the tern's print is less than a third the length of the gull's. See note 4 below.
4. The herring gull is a common bird along the Atlantic Coast and on inland lakes and rivers. The print shows front toes quite clearly, the fourth or hind toe, being somewhat above the heel of the foot, making only a slight impression.
5. As the wood duck nests in a hollow tree, it is provided

with unusually long claws to help it in climbing. They show in the print and serve to distinguish the print of the wood duck from that of other ducks.

6. The prints of the different species of ducks are much alike (except those of the wood duck, see note 5 above) varying only slightly in size. The mallard was selected as representative of the group because it is probably the best known of our wild ducks.

7. The Canada goose may be seen in the eastern half of the United States only during the spring and fall migrations and throughout the winter. The prints are similar to those of the ducks except that they are larger in size. When walking, the goose toes-in quite decidedly.

8. The flamingo was once a regular winter visitor to the extremity of the Florida coast but now may be seen there only occasionally. (The flamingoes at the Bok Sanctuary and at the Hialeah Race Track are captive birds.) The print of the flamingo is similar to that of the goose (see note 7 above) except that its middle toe appears to be somewhat larger. Also its prints are not toed-in as they are in the track of the goose.

9. The cormorant is a large dark water bird readily recognized by its very blackness. Its print is somewhat similar to that of the pelican except that it is smaller. See note 10 below.

10. The pelican is a strange, weird creature in appearance and is familiar to everyone, at least by name. Its print is similar to that of the cormorant but larger.

11. During the fall migration, the semi-palmated sandpiper may be seen in vast numbers at various places along the coast as well as along the sandy or muddy margins of inland lakes, ponds, and streams. The name "semi-palmated" refers to the partially webbed

toes; the partial web showing between the outer and middle toes. The toe marks are exceptionally slender. The walking track pattern shows the prints somewhat toed-in.

12. The prints of the semi-palmated plover may be seen in the sand of the sea beach and in the mud of mud-flats during the migratory flights. They look much like a small "y." The outer and middle toes are close together and the bird toes-in when walking. This plover is one of the many birds of the beach and may be seen in flocks that number forty to fifty individuals. Sometimes the plovers may be seen alone, at other times in company with other shore birds.

13. The spotted sandpiper is undoubtedly the most widely distributed of our shore birds; certainly it is the best known and to some extent that is because of its curious habit of teetering up and down between steps when walking. Its prints and tracks may be seen in the mud of the margins of most lakes and streams throughout the summer. The toes leave a rather delicate imprint and there is a web between the outer and middle toes. The bird toes-in slightly both when walking and when running.

14. The Wilson's phalarope breeds in a small area in the Midwest where its prints may be seen in the wet meadows and grassy marshes during the summer. During the fall migration it may be observed along the Atlantic Coast. It winters in South America.

15. The greater yellow-legs with its long bright yellow legs is a shy wild bird that may be seen only during its spring and fall migratory flights and throughout the winter only along the southern coasts. The prints show the toes widely spread, the outer toe being closer to the middle toe than the inner.

16. The hind toe of the willet, a strikingly marked shore bird, makes only a slight imprint in the sand of the sea beach or in the mud of a mud-flat. The track shows that the prints are slightly toed-in.

17. The grebe is essentially a water bird and ventures on land but rarely and then only during the nesting season. Like the loon (see note 1 above), it also is clumsy on land and walks with difficulty, leaving a sort of halting track in the mud of the marshy pond or lake.

18. The coot, a clumsy looking bird with a somewhat silly look on its face, is chiefly a freshwater species though it may sometimes be seen in the salt marshes. Its strange lobed toes leave an unusual and a quite distinctive scalloped imprint in the wet mud of a marshy pond or slough.

19. The flicker, the most abundant of our woodpeckers, is probably also the best known woodpecker. Its prints show two front toes and two hind toes which are characteristic of the woodpecker and serve to identify the bird. Though other members of the woodpecker family also have two front toes and two hind toes the flicker is the only one apt to be seen on the ground.

20. The piping plover is a bird of the sandy shore and its prints may be seen there. They can be identified because the inner toe is shorter than the others.

21. The sanderling frequents the sand flats and outer beaches where it can be seen alternately chasing the retreating waves and then hurrying to escape them as they return to the shore. Its prints may be confused with those of the piping plover but in the prints of the sanderling the middle toe seems to be closer to the inner toe than the outer. It migrates along the Atlantic Coast.

22. The English or house sparrow, which is not a sparrow but a weaver bird, is familiar to practically everyone. Its prints show the middle and inner toes usually close together. The prints of the song sparrow, probably the best known of our native sparrows, are similar.

23. The killdeer is the common bird of plowed fields and pasture lands. The middle toe, being longer than either the outer or inner toes, makes a deeper impression in the mud or sand. The outer toe is closer to the middle toe than to the inner toe. Sometimes the hind toe fails to register in the print. The track shows the prints distinctly toed-in.

24. The woodcock usually haunts low, wooded bottom lands in spring and early summer. Later, in August, it resorts to pastures and cornfields and then during the migratory flights in fall, it is more often seen in wooded uplands. The print of the woodcock shows the toes as being long and slender with the outer and hind toes in line with each other. The joints of the middle and inner toes are enlarged. When walking, the bird places the feet diagonally ahead of each other, producing a sort of zigzag track pattern. Holes, called borings, made in search of earthworms are frequently to be seen in the mud and are a characteristic feature of the track.

25. This is the familiar quail of the farming country whose call is a welcome sound of spring and summer. The prints sometimes show the inner and outer toes widely spread. The outer toe is much the same length as the middle toe and the hind toe is quite small. The walking track shows a toed-in pattern.

26. When a hint of snow is in the air, the junco appears about our dooryards and in the neighboring weedy

fields where its prints may be seen in the snow throughout the winter. The paired prints show that the bird hops as it moves over the ground.

27. During the winter the horned lark may often be observed in numbers running or walking over snow-covered fields. The nail of the hind toe, being unusually long—almost as long as the middle toe—usually drags and this in the prints makes the hind toe appear abnormally long. The prints make an alternate track pattern.

28. The prints of the Wilson's snipe, known for its peculiar song-flight to all who frequent the outdoors, resemble those of the woodcock except for being slightly larger. In its track its borings (the snipe like the woodcock also plunges its bill into the mud for earthworms) are not quite so prominent as in the woodcock's track.

29. The mourning dove is a bird of the open country and is usually seen in grassy fields and grain-fields. In the print the middle toe appears longer than the outer and inner toes which are equally spaced and about the same length. When walking, the dove places one foot ahead of the other and toes-in slightly. Its print is similar to the pigeon's except that the middle toe is not bent in as much.

30. The ruffed grouse is a woodland bird and is usually not found far from cover. It is usually not seen until it springs into the air with a sudden and startling whir. In its summer prints the toes are slender compared with those in winter when its toes grow horn-like marginal fringes that serve as snowshoes and enable the bird to walk upon the surface of the snow. The hind toe registers only slightly in the print.

31. This familiar bird, one of the best known of our avian fauna yet paradoxically one that most people know

very little about, is not a robin but a thrush. If a robin is observed on the ground it will be seen to take a number of hops and then run in the manner of any ground bird. This hopping and running is clearly seen in the track pattern, the hopping indicated by the pairing of the prints and the running because the prints are arranged in a single file.

32. During the summer, the Virginia rail frequents the fresh-water marshes but in the autumn it may be seen in grain or stubble fields. In May and June it gives voice to a series of grunting notes that are not unlike those of a hungry pig. Its prints are similar to those of the sandhill crane (see note 41 below) but only about half their size. Also the front toes do not appear to spread as readily as those of the crane.

33. The meadowlark, a bird of the grassy field and meadow where it may often be flushed when walking through the tall grass, makes a walking track pattern that can be identified by its alternating prints.

34. The adjective pigeon-toed seems to have come from the pigeon's habit of toeing-in when walking though actually the pigeon toes-in much less noticeably than many other birds. The domestic pigeon has become feral and in some places has become established as a wild species more usually known as the rock dove.

35. East of the Mississippi, the burrowing owl is limited to the prairies of Florida. Owls make a rather odd-shaped imprint in sand, mud or snow which can be said to be x-shaped. Unlike most owls, the burrowing owl is diurnal in habit and during the day may often be seen sitting on the ground or perched on a fence post.

36. The normal habitat of the prairie chicken, a scratching hen-like bird, is the prairies and brushy grasslands.

Its print is about the size of a small domestic hen but since the toes widen at the base the print looks different from that in the poultry-yard. The prairie chicken does not spread its toes as wide as other members of the grouse family nor does it toe-in as do the others.

37. The odd-shaped prints characteristic of the owls (see note 35 above) may often be seen in the snow, and together with bits of fur or feathers, are evidence that the great horned owl has hunted successfully.

38. The starling has become so well established in our country and is so common in our cities and towns that it should be as familiar as the robin or English sparrow, yet there are many who do not know the bird. The toes appear to be too long in proportion to the rest of the print. The track pattern is characteristic of a walking bird.

39. The wood thrush is usually an inhabitant of the cool woodlands, but after the nesting season it may be seen in a wooded hillside or thicket and sometimes in the vicinity of human habitations. Its prints and track pattern are similar to those of the robin though the prints are somewhat larger.

40. The ring-necked pheasant, a large chicken-like bird imported from Europe and now fairly well established in the north, is essentially a bird of farming country but during the winter often appears on the outskirts of villages and towns. In the print its middle toe is seen to be the longest, its inner toe the shortest. The track pattern is a straight and narrow trail, the middle toe making an almost straight line. There is no toe-ing-in.

41. The sandhill crane, like many other species, was far more common at one time than now. It is now rare

east of the Mississippi and is to be found in only a few localities. The toes of its print are widely spread with just an indication of the hind toe a little to one side.

42. Probably no bird has been more written about or talked about than the crow. Little need be said about it here except that its prints are often found in sand, mud, and snow. Its "swollen" toes leave a print that is distinctive and readily recognized. The inner and middle toes are close together and the track pattern often shows a foot drag. Sometimes the imprint of the wing tips shows in the track.

43. The green heron, the smallest and most widely distributed of the true herons, is, unlike other herons, a solitary species and usually nests alone, though sometimes a dozen or more pairs may be found living together. Its print is a miniature of the great blue heron's (see note 44 below) being about one-third its size.

44. Next to the sandhill crane, the great blue heron is the largest of our wading birds. Often seen alone and hence regarded as a solitary bird it lives in communities during the breeding season and during the migratory flights it often flies in large flocks. Its prints are similar to those of the bittern (see note 49 below) but about 3 inches longer. Its stride, too, is greater than that of the bittern's and it toes-in somewhat.

45. The prints of the domestic chicken show the imprint of its peculiar toenails which are adapted for scratching and raking.

46. The Florida gallinule, a bird with the appearance of a chicken and often called water-hen, is equally at home wading among the reeds or swimming in the

open water. The toes in its print are slender with the hind toe almost equal in length to the middle toe.

47. The black-crowned night heron, as its name implies, is a bird of the night; its harsh cry a familiar sound in the dusk of a summer's evening as it issues from a wooded swamp. Its print and track are similar to the great blue heron's but smaller.

48. The turkey is the largest of our game birds and its print is most distinctive because of its size. The three front toes are rather thick and the tip of the hind toe leaves an imprint off to one side in the print. The middle toe is somewhat curved inward. This enhances the toeing effect of the track pattern.

49. The bittern is well-known for its vocal performance or "boom" which can be heard for quite a distance. The bird is something of a hermit and an odd character that excites our curiosity. Its print and track are similar to those of the great blue heron (see note 44 above) except for size and depth of imprint.

PART III

TRACKS
OF
REPTILES

Prints and Tracks of Reptiles

Snakes, turtles, and lizards, as well as alligators, leave their prints in sand and mud as do the mammals and birds. On a dusty road the track of a turtle, perhaps that of the snapper, may often be seen, evidence that it plodded along that way, shell held high and with slow and short steps leaving two curious parallel rows of prints, spaced about the width of its shell. Sometimes a tail mark may be part of the track.

On the muddy shore of a pond the prints of the painted turtle as well as those of the wood turtle are often to be seen though the tracks of the wood turtle may be found elsewhere since the animal wanders about a great deal. On southern beaches the prints and tracks of the gopher tortoise are fairly common; less so are those of the logger-head turtle.

Snakes move over the ground with an undulating move-ment of the body from side to side. Wherever the ground is soft enough to take an impression a sinous furrow is plowed, and if the movement is in sand, a series of slightly curved hillocks of sand is piled up at the back of each curve. These hillocks are used by the snake to aid in its forward progression and from this we can tell the direction of travel.

Lizards that live on the desert leave their prints and

tracks in the sand as they hunt for food or hurry to escape an enemy. Those that inhabit the woodlands write their signatures in the mud and sand when it is soft enough to take an imprint.

On the muddy shores of southern ponds the prints of the alligator are not an uncommon sight. The track, readily identified by the clawed prints and the groove of the tail between them, is a deeply rutted winding path and often leads to the "hole" in which the alligator lives; the "hole" being a small, deep, depression filled with water and surrounded by growing vegetation.

PART IV

TRACKS
OF
AMPHIBIANS

Prints and Tracks
of Amphibians

Most of us have seen a toad hop and we usually think of the toad as hopping when it wants to get from one place to another. But when unmolested and in no hurry, it walks. Toads are frequent inhabitants of our gardens. After a rainfall their prints may sometimes be seen in the mud. Occasionally their prints and track may be observed in the sand of a country road, where the little animal left evidence of its leisurely pace in the form of a ,walking track.

Unlike the toad, frogs seem only to hop. On the sandy or muddy shore of a pond or stream the prints of the leopard and pickerel frogs may frequently be seen throughout the summer. Less often may be seen the large prints of the bullfrog which remains for the most part in the water, coming out on land only infrequently. During the spring mating season the tiny prints of the spring peeper may occasionally be observed in the shore mud of a pond or pool.

In moist woodlands and similar damp places the prints and tracks of salamanders may sometimes be discovered, particularly after a rainfall. The prints and tracks of the toad and several frogs have been illustrated in this book to show how they appear in their natural surroundings.

PART V

TRACKS OF INSECTS AND OTHER INVERTEBRATES

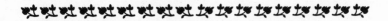

Prints and Tracks of
Insects and Other Invertebrates

Different kinds of insects leave their prints in sand, dust, and mud. A few of them have been illustrated in this book. The six legs of insects, some pushing, others pulling, frequently leave a curious and complex series of prints. Consider, for instance, the track pattern of a grasshopper, a cricket, and a beetle and you will find that the patterns show a certain similarity. The backward pointing mark is made by the hind leg as it trails behind the insect and the cross mark by the middle leg. Note that each print cluster consists of three parts, the three parts representing the three feet on each side. Grasshopper and beetle prints are fairly common on sand dunes but they may be observed elsewhere as well as on a sandy or dusty road.

Every animal that travels over the ground leaves an impression of some kind if the ground is soft enough. Thus, after a rainfall you are likely to find the trails of earthworms in the wet mud of the garden, the rain having forced them out of their burrows. And on the sea beach you are sure to find bands of dots where the many-footed crab moved sideways over the sand and the winding trail of a periwinkle as it moved about in a seemingly aimless fashion. These are only a few of the many kinds of prints and tracks you will see outdoors, especially if you keep an eye out for them in likely places.

73

APPENDIXES

Where to Find Prints and Tracks

To say that prints and tracks of animals may be found everywhere is a slight exaggeration and yet it is essentially true. It is rather difficult to think of a place where some animal may not have wandered at some time and left its calling card as proof of having been there. Prints and tracks may even be seen on a rocky cliff.

A sandy country road, the muddy bank of a pond or stream, a dusty hollow underneath an overhanging rock ledge, a sand dune, the wet beach of the seashore are all places where prints and tracks may be found—even your own backyard should not be overlooked. And when snow covers the ground the neighboring field, the more distant meadow, and the nearby woodland reveal the presence of many animals whose existence was probably never suspected. If you wander about the countryside by day and catch only a glimpse of a squirrel or rabbit, you are likely to think that mammals have almost disappeared. Actually they have more than held their own and even on the outskirts of a large city, a surprising number are present though few of us see them. The mammals are not the only ones to see for there are birds, reptiles, amphibians and many others. Even though many species are merely relics of the past and others are on the verge of becoming so, the animal world is still well populated.

Recording and Preserving Prints and Tracks

Animals autographs can be saved for future reference and study or simply for the mere pleasure of doing so. The project of preserving them can be made into an interesting hobby.

Photographing Prints and Tracks: Usually photographs of prints and tracks showing details can only be made when the sun leaves definite shadows, in the early morning or in late afternoon. Unfortunately, the light is often not bright enough at this time of the day for good pictures. However, fairly good pictures can be made at other times with a little practice. For snow pictures a yellow filter should be used to produce good contrasts.

Making Drawings: Anyone with some sketching ability can make drawings of prints and tracks in a notebook. Later a more permanent record can be made in ink on bristol board or a good grade of drawing paper, on sheets of an 8½ by 11 inch size which can be kept in a loose-leaf binder.

A pocket tape measure is a necessity for measuring the individual prints as well as the distance between successive sets of prints; that is, the stride of a walking track pattern and the leap of a running track pattern. The drawings may be made either actual size or to scale but in any event they should be carefully made. Needless to say they should be labeled with the name of the animal as well as the date, location, and the medium in which they were found.

Making Plaster Casts: An excellent method of preserving prints is to make plaster casts. Eventually an entire collection can be built up. Several substances are used in making casts but plaster of paris seems to be the best. All the equipment needed is a container in which to carry the plaster, another for water, and a third in which to mix the two as well as a spoon for handling the plaster and for mixing it with the water.

When using plaster of paris it is essential to get the right mixture. If it is too thick it will not run into the print evenly and enter all the crevices so that details of the print will not be caught, and it will harden too quickly and set before the print has been completely filled. On the other hand if it is too thin it will run all over the print and take too long to harden. A little experimenting will probably be necessary to find the proper consistency which may differ from time to time according to the temperature and other factors.

For obvious reasons it is easier to make a cast in mud or even sand than in snow or dust. Before allowing the plaster to flow into the print it is advisable to place a "collar" of heavy paper or cardboard around the print to contain the plaster which should overflow the margins of the print so that the edges and claw marks and other details will show up in the cast.

When the plaster has hardened, the print should then be carefully cut out with a knife and lifted from a point well underneath. Any mud or sand clinging to the print should be washed off with water, using an old toothbrush for the purpose. If water is not available loose mud or sand may be brushed off and the remainder later washed off.

The cast thus made may be likened to the negative of a photograph. To make a positive cast, grease the negative, fit a cardboard collar around it, and then fill with a mixture of plaster and water. When the plaster has hardened, the second cast can then be removed. This second impression will be the positive and show the sunken impression of the animal's foot as it appeared in the mud or sand.

Though making casts of prints in mud and sand is not too difficult, a little practice is helpful. To prepare a cast from a print in dust requires extra care; for instance, the plaster should be poured into the print as close to the print as possible. In other words, it should not be allowed to drop in so that it will splash about and distort the print. To prepare a cast from a print in snow is also not easy, and is impossible if the temperature is above freezing, since the liquid mixture of plaster and water is apt to melt the snow and make the print unrecognizable. One way of avoiding this, however, is to spray the print with enough water from an atomizer to form a thin coating of ice throughout the print. It will then retain the plaster mixture until it has had time to harden.

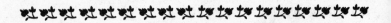

Reading the Stories That
Prints and Tracks Tell

The prints and tracks of animals reveal much of their anatomy, their relationship to their environment, and their habits and behavior. Prints that show essentially only toe marks indicate that the animals who make them have a need for speed, either for the purpose of capturing their food or to escape from their enemies. On the other hand prints that show the entire foot are likely those of animals that have no need to travel swiftly and are in the habit of walking on the flat of their feet; the so-called "flat-foots." Then there are the animals that walk or run on their toenails, the hoofed animals in other words, such as the horse, cow, sheep, goat, deer, etc.

Prints that show partially webbed feet are evidence that animals having such feet live in marshy places and must be equipped in some way to prevent them from sinking into the mud. The sandpiper is a case in point. Prints that show fully webbed feet indicate that their makers live a more or less aquatic existence and that such feet are used in propelling them through the water. The beaver, whose webbed hind feet show in the prints, is a familiar example.

Tree climbers have well developed claws to aid them in climbing. Claw marks are a characteristic feature of their prints. Claw marks that show exceptionally well developed claws, such as those of the badger, serve notice that the animal is in the habit of digging. Cats, too, have claws but since they are used in hunting and are an essential part of the animal's equipment for survival, they are always sheathed and withdrawn when moving over the ground so that they will not be worn down and dulled by the wear and tear of the trail. Hence they do not show in the cat's prints. The cat's track show that the animal is a stalker. The hind feet are placed in the steps of the front feet, which makes for a silent tread, and the prints are in an almost straight line. Except for their smaller size, the prints and tracks of the domestic cat are like those of its wild relatives; lion, tiger, leopard, and panther. In a sense the cat is a direct link with the jungle.

Unlike the cat, the dog, except for occasional digging, has no particular use for claws, and since they are not withdrawn when it is walking and running they are often a feature of its prints. And speaking of the dog, it is less suspicious than its feral cousin the wolf or coyote. Thus its track will show a more or less direct approach to an object that may have aroused its interest whereas that of the wolf or coyote will show that these animals are more circumspect. In a somewhat similar manner the track of the mink reveals that it is less wary than its relative, the weasel. The mink will usually explore any hole or burrow as soon as it comes upon it whereas the weasel will make several circles of inspection before it decides to enter.

Animals with long hind legs, such as the squirrels and rabbits, bound when they move over the ground, the hind feet usually coming down together and touching the ground ahead of the front feet, hence their prints fall in groups. Animals with short legs and wide heavy bodies have a tendency to toe-in. Animals with long slender bodies bound along when in a hurry producing a track with groups of four prints. Both groups when not in a hurry leave a track with many prints rather close together.

Quite frequently a track will suddenly show a variation in gait which may or may not be a story in itself. Sometimes on a desert a series of prints may stop abruptly and in the absence of other prints be puzzling until it is remembered that some lizards dive into the sand for shelter and "swim" through the sand beneath the surface.

The tracks of an animal are often a clue to its feeding habits. I recall one time following the erratic course of a cottontail in the snow as the animal searched for rose hips and other berries and stopped here and there to feed on the bark and twigs of small trees and bushes. Eventually the track led to a clump of sumacs to which it is particularly partial. Sometimes the track of a mouse will end in a series of blurred prints in snow that is stained red; one need hardly wonder what happened.

The tail mark, a characteristic feature of some tracks, is often an indication of the animal's behavior. Most mammals drag their tails only when moving very slowly. When the need for speed becomes paramount the tail is usually raised clear of the ground. However, when a fox leaves a tail mark it is invariably a sign that it has become tired, perhaps from being pursued by a pack of dogs.

If we learn to read them and to interpret what they tell us, the prints and tracks of animals can tell us much; not only about the kind of animal that made them but also its habits and behavior under normal conditions or in time of stress. The stories they tell can be as fascinating as those you find in a book but first you have to learn how to read them.

Drawings of Tracks

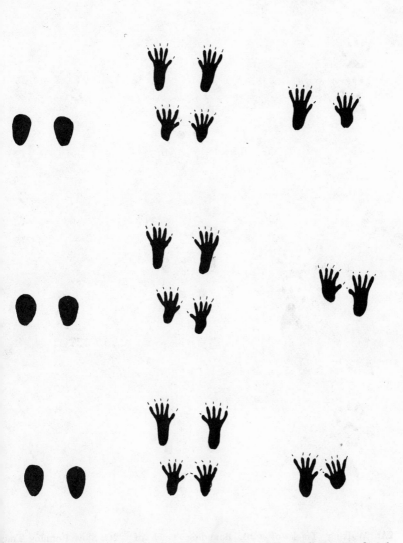

. Speeding Track of
eld Mouse in Snow.
atural size: FF ¼″ x
″, HF ⅜″ x ½″, 3″
ps.

1B. Running Track of
Raccoon in Mud. Natural
size: FF 2½″ x 3″, HF
2½″ x 4″, leaps to 20″.

1C. Walking Track of
Raccoon in Mud. Natural
size: FF 2½″ x 3″, HF
2½″ x 4″, 7″ stride.

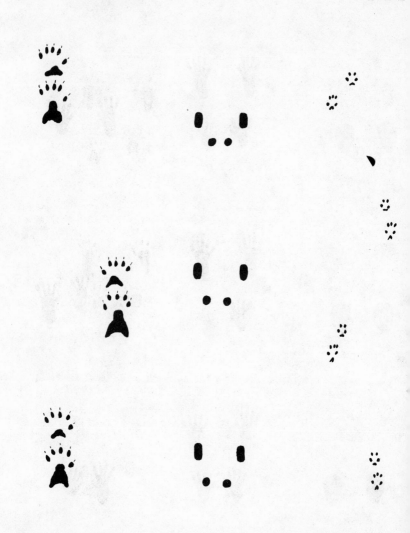

2A. Walking Track of Fisher in Mud. Natural size: FF 3″ x 2½″, HF 3″ x 2½″, 13″ stride.

2B. Bounding Track of Shrew in Snow Without Tail Mark. Natural size: FF 3⁄16″ x 3⁄16″, HF 3⁄16″ x 3⁄8″, 1¾″ leaps.

2C. Slow Running Track of House Mouse in Mud. Natural size: FF ¼″ x ¼″, HF ¼″ x 3⁄8″, 6¼ to 7½″ leaps.

Walking Track of Striped Skunk
Mud. Natural size: FF 1½″ x 2″,
1½″ x 2½″, 5″ stride.

3B. Bounding Track of Spotted Skunk
in Mud. Natural size: FF 1″ x 1¼″,
HF 1″ x 1½″, 4″ to 14″ leaps.

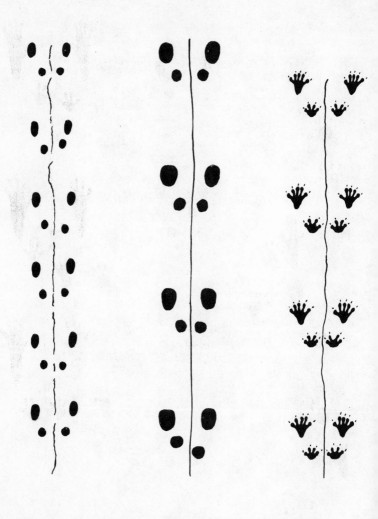

4A. Bounding Track of Shrew in Snow. Showing Tail Mark. Natural size: FF ³⁄₁₆″ x ³⁄₁₆″, HF ³⁄₁₆″ x 3⅛″, 1¾″ leaps.

4B. Bounding Track of Deer Mouse in Snow. Natural Size: FF ¼″ x ¼″, HF ⅜″ x ½″, 3″ leaps.

4C. Bounding Track of Deer Mouse in Sand. Natural size: FF ¼″ x ¼″, HF ⅜″ x ½″, 3″ leaps.

PLATE 5   91

5A. Slow Hopping Track of Jumping Mouse in Mud. Natural size: FF ¼″ x ½″, HF ½″ x ¼″, 2½″ leaps.

5B. Running Track of House Mouse in Snow. Natural size: FF ¼″ x 1¼″, HF ¼″ x ⅜″, 6¼″ to 7½″ leaps.

5C. Hopping Track of Brown Rat in Snow with Tail Mark. Natural size: FF ½″ x ½″, HF ½″ x 1½″, 4″ leaps.

6A. Running Track of Mink in Mud. Natural size: FF 1½" x 1½", HF 1½" x 1¾", 11" leaps.

6B. Walking Track of House Cat in Snow. Natural size: FF 1⅛" x 1⅛", HF 1⅛" x 1⅛", 6" stride.

6C. Walking Track Bobcat in Snow. Natur size: FF 1¾" x 1⅞ HF 1¾" x 1⅞", 1 stride.

PLATE 7 93

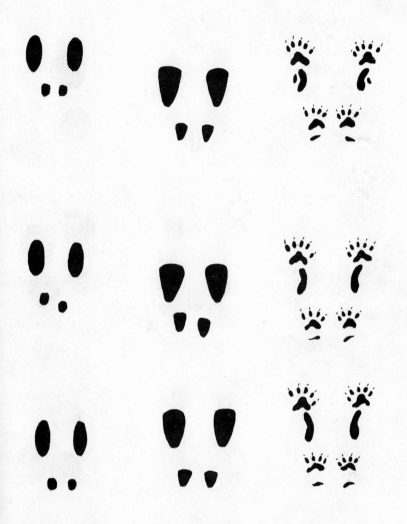

7A. Bounding Track of Flying Squirrel in Snow. Natural size: FF ½" x ½", HF ¾" x 1¾", 11" to 29" leaps.

7B. Bounding Track of Red Squirrel in Snow. Natural size: FF ½" x ¾", HF 1" x 1¾", 8" to 30" leaps.

7C. Bounding Track of Gray Squirrel in Mud. Natural size: FF 1" x 1½", HF 1¼" x 2½", 24" to 36" leaps.

8A. Slow Running Track of Deer Mouse in Mud. Natural size: FF ¼" x ¼", HF ⅜" x ½", 3" leaps.

8B. Walking Track of Woodchuck in Sand and Mud. Natural size: FF 1¼" x 1½", HF 1¼" x 1¾", 3½" stride.

8C. Walking Track of Dog in Snow. Natural size: FF 2¾" x 2½", HF 2½" x 2", stride up to 10".

PLATE 9   95

9A. Galloping Track of Black Bear in Mud. Natural size: FF 3″ x 4″, HF 4″ x 7″, to 37″ leaps.

9B. Walking Track of Coyote in Mud. Natural size: FF 1¾″ x 2½″, HF 1½″ x 2¼″, 14″ stride.

9C. Running Track of Coyote in Mud. Natural size: FF 1¾″ x 2½″, HF 1½″ x 2¼″, 16″ leaps.

PLATE 1

10A. Running Track of Chipmunk in Mud. Natural size: FF ½″ x ⅜″, HF ¾″ x 1¼″, 6″ leaps.

10B. Speeding Track of Cottontail in Snow. Natural size: FF 1″ x 1″, HF 1¾″ x 3½″, leaps to 7′.

10C. Speeding Track of Meadow Mouse in Sand. Natural size: FF ½″ x ½″, HF ½″ x ¾″, 9″ leaps.

PLATE 11   97

11A. Walking Track of Porcupine in Snow. Natural size: FF 1½″ x 2¾″, HF 2″ x 3½″, stride less than 1′.

11B. Walking Track of Badger in Sand or Mud. Natural size: FF 2″ x 2″, HF 2″ x 1¾″, 6″ to 12″ stride.

11C. Walking Track of Black Bear in Sand or Mud. Natural size: FF 3″ x 4″, HF 4″ x 7″, 12″ stride.

PLATE 12

12A. Walking Track of Rice Rat in Mud. Natural size: FF ½″ x ½″, HF ¾″ x ⅞″.

12B. Walking Track of Armadillo in Mud. Natural size: FF 1⅜″ x 1¾″, HF 1½″ x 2⅛″.

12C. Walking Track of Marten in Snow. Natural size: FF ¾″ x 1¼″, HF 1⅛″ x 1⅞″, 9″ stride.

PLATE 13 99

13A. Bounding Track of Gray Squirrel in Snow. Natural size: FF 1″ x 1½″, HF 1¼″ x 2½″, 24″ to 36″ leaps.

13B. Bounding Track of Fox Squirrel in Mud. Natural size: FF 1″ x 1¾″, HF 1½″ x 2¾″, leaps to 36″.

PLATE 14

14A. Walking Track of House Cat in Mud. Natural size: FF 1⅛″ x 1⅛″, HF 1⅛″ x 1⅛″, 6″ stride.

14B. Galloping Track of House Cat in Snow. Natural size: FF 1⅛″ x 1⅛″, HF 1⅛″ x 1⅛″, 32″ leaps.

14C. Walking Track of Bobcat in Mud. Natural size: FF 1¾″ x 1⅞″, HF 1¾″ x 1⅞″, 14″ stride.

PLATE 15 101

15A. Walking Track of Long-tailed Weasel in Mud. Natural size: FF ¾″ x ½″, HF ⅝″ x 1″.

15B. Walking Track of Spotted Skunk in Mud. Natural size: FF 1″ x 1¼″, HF 1″ x 1½″, 5″ stride.

15C. Running Track of Badger in Mud. Natural size: FF 2″ x 2″, HF 2″ x 1¾″, 6″ leaps.

16A. Walking Track of Marten in Mud. Natural size: FF ¾″ x 1¼″, HF 1⅛″ x 1⅞″.

16B. Walking Track of Armadillo in Mud. Natural size: FF 1⅜″ x 1¾″, HF 1½″ x 2⅛″.

16C. Running Track of Red Squirrel in Mud. Natural size: FF ½″ x ¾″, HF 1″ x 1¾″, 8″ to 10″ leaps.

PLATE 17

17A. Walking Track of Beaver in Mud. Natural size: FF 2½″ x 3½″, HF 5½″ x 7″, 16″ stride.

17B. Galloping Track of Striped Skunk in Mud. Natural size: FF 1½″ x 2″, HF 1½″ x 2½″, 12″ leaps.

PLATE 18

18A. Walking Track of Red Fox in Mud. Natural size: FF 2″ x 2½″, HF 1¾″ x 2″, 8″ to 18″ stride.

18B. Running Track of Red Fox in Snow. Natural size: FF 2″ x 2½″, HF 1¾″ x 2″.

18C. Walking Track of Gray Fox in Snow. Natural size: FF 1½″ x 1⅞″, HF 1½″ x 1¾″, 6″ to 16″ stride.

PLATE 19 105

19A. Bounding Track of Weasel in Snow Without Tail Mark. Natural size: FF ½″ x ½″, HF ⅜″ x ⅝″, 8″ to 12″ bounds.

19B. Walking Track of Opossum in Mud. Natural size: FF 1¾″ x 1½″, HF 1¼″ x 1¾″, 12″ stride.

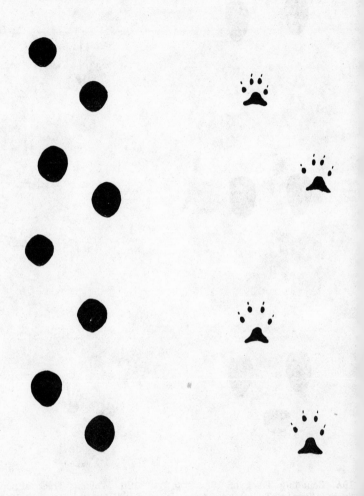

20A. Walking Track of Mink in Snow. Natural size: FF 1½″ x 1½″, HF 1½″ x 1¾″.

20B. Walking Track of Mink in M Natural size: FF 1½″ x 1½″, 1½″ x 1¾″.

PLATE 21

107

21A. Bounding Track of River Otter in Snow Without Tail Mark. Natural size: FF 2″ x 2″, HF 2½″ x 2¾″, 20″ leaps.

21B. Walking Track of River Otter in Snow. Natural size: FF 2″ x 2″, HF 2½″ x 2¾″.

PLATE 22

22A. Bounding Track of Mink in Snow With Tail Mark. Natural size: FF 1½" x 1½", HF 1½" x 1¾", 12" to 23" leaps.

22B. Bounding Track of Mink in Snow Without Tail Mark. Natural size: FF 1½" x 1½", HF 1½" x 1¾", 12" to 23" leaps.

22C. Walking Track of Coyote in Snow. Natural size: FF 1¾" x 2½", HF 1½" x 2¼", 14" stride.

PLATE 23

23A. Walking Track of Brown Rat in Mud. Natural size: FF ½″ x ½″, HF ½″ x 1½″, 3″ stride.

23B. Walking Track of Shrew in Snow. Natural size: FF ³⁄₁₆″ x ³⁄₁₆″, HF ³⁄₁₆″ x ⅜″.

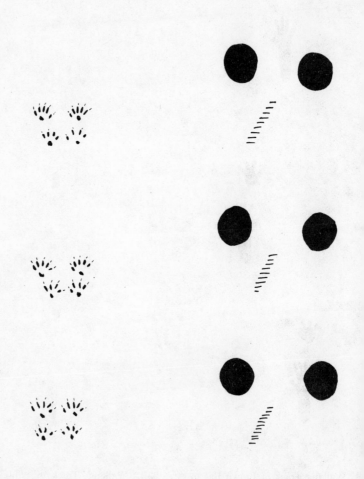

24A. Running Track of Deer Mouse in Snow. Natural size: FF ¼″ x ¼″, HF ⅜″ x ½″, 3″ leaps.

24B. Bounding Track of River Otter in Snow With Tail Mark. Natural size: FF 2″ x 2″, HF 2½″ x 2¾″, 20″ leaps.

PLATE 25   111

25A. Slow Hopping Track of Varying Hare in Snow. Natural size: FF 3" x 3", HF 3½" x 6½", leaps to 2'.

25B. Walking Track of Porcupine in Mud. Natural size: FF 1½" x 2¾", HF 2" x 3½", stride less than 1'.

PLATE 26

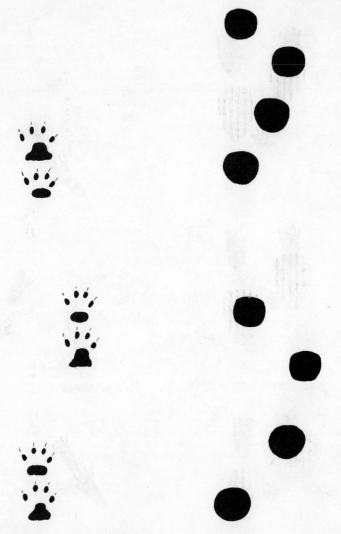

26A. Walking Track of Dog in Mud. Natural size: FF 2¾" x 2½", HF 2½" x 2".

26B. Galloping Track of Dog in Snow. Natural size: FF 2¾" x 2½", HF 2½" x 2".

PLATE 27   113

A. Bounding Track of Fisher in ...ow. Natural size: FF 3″ x 2½″, F 3″ x 2½″, 26″ leaps.

27B. Walking Track of Wood Rat in Mud. Natural size: FF ½″ x ¾″, HF ⅝″ x 1⅞″, 3″ stride.

28A. Running Track of River Otter in Mud. Natural size: FF 2″ x 2″, HF 2½″ x 2¾″, 15″ to 22″ leaps.

28B. Walking Track of Harvest Mous in Mud. Natural size: FF ¼″ x ¼′ HF ³⁄₁₆″ x ¼″, 1″ stride.

PLATE 29   115

29A. Bounding Track of Weasel in Snow With Tail Mark. Natural size: ¾" x ½", HF ⅝" x 1", 12" to leaps.

29B. Bounding Track of Marten in Snow. Natural size: FF ¾" x 1¼", HF 1⅛" x 1⅞", 9" to 46" leaps.

30A. Walking Track of Meadow Mouse in Mud. Natural size: FF ½" x ½", HF ½" x ¾", 1½" stride.

30B. Speeding Track of Wood Rat Mud. Natural size: FF ½" x ¾ HF ⅝" x 1⅞", 7" to 8" leaps.

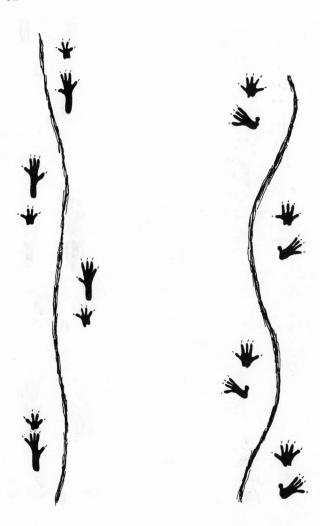

A. Walking Track of Muskrat in
ud With Tail Mark. Natural size:
¼″ x ¼″, HF ³⁄₁₆″ x ¼″, 1″
ide.

31B. Walking Track of Opossum in
Snow With Tail Mark. Natural size:
FF 1¾″ x 1½″, HF 1¼″ x 1¾″,
12″ stride.

32A. Walking Track of Grey Squirrel in Mud. Natural size: FF 1″ x 1½″, HF 1¼″ x 2½″.

32B. Hopping Track of Brown Rat in Snow Without Tail Mark. Natural size: FF ½″ x ½″, HF ½″ x 1½″, 3″ stride.

PLATE 33   119

33A. Running Track of Prairie Dog in Sand or Mud. Natural size: FF ¾″ x 1″, HF 1″ x 1¼″, 3¾″ to 6½″ leaps.

33B. Walking Track of Cotton Rat in Mud. Natural size: FF ½″ x ¾″, HF ¾″ x 1″, 1¼″ stride.

34A. Walking Track of Sheep in Mud. Natural size: HP 2½″.

34B. Galloping Track of White-tailed Deer in Snow. Natural size: HP 2½″ to 3″, 6′ leaps.

34C. Walking Track of White-tailed Deer in Mud. Natural size: HP 2½″ to 3″. Stride 18″

PLATE 35   121

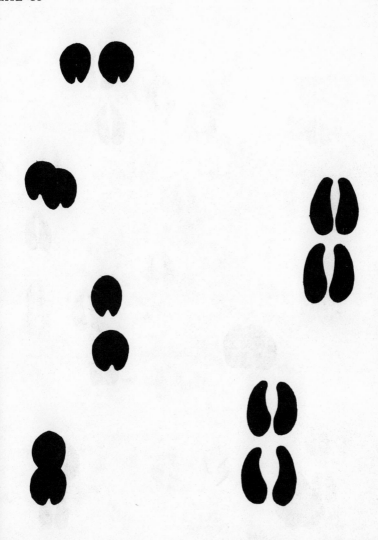

35A. Walking Track of Horse in Mud
Sand. Stride 25".

35B. Walking Track of Goat in Mud
or Sand. Natural size: HP 2⅝", 15"
stride.

36A. Walking Track of Cow in Mud.
Natural size: HP 4″, 17″ to 21″ stride.

36B. Walking Track of Pig in Mud.
Natural size: HP 3″, 10″ to 11″ stride.

PLATE 37   123

A. Greater Yellow-legs. Natural size: 2⅛″ long.

37E. Double-crested Cormorant. Natural size: 4″ long.

B. Loon. Natural Size: 4″ long.

37F. Ruffed Grouse with Winter Fringes on Toes.

C. Grebe. Natural size: long.

D. Pelican. Natural size: 5″ long.

37G. Great Horned Owl in Snow. Natural size: 2½″ long.

37H. Trotting Track of Moose on Hard Snow. Natural size: HP 7″, 43″ stride.

38A. Wild Turkey. Natural size: 5″ long.

38D. Herring Gull. Natural size: 3½″ long.

38G. Florida Gallinu Natural size: 4″ long.

38B. American Bittern. Natural size: 5″ long.

38E. Ring-necked Pheasant. Natural size: 3½″ long.

38H. Green Heron. N ural size: 3″ long.

38C. Semi - palmated Sandpiper. Natural size: ⅞″ long.

38F. Great Blue Heron. Natural size: 8″ long.

38I. Flamingo. Natu size: 4″ long.

PLATE 39

39A. Meadowlark. Natural size: 2″ long.

39B. Sanderling. Natural size: ⅞″ long.

39C. Common Tern. Natural size: 1″ long.

39D. Junco. Natural size: ½″.

39E. English Sparrow. Natural size: 1⅛″ long.

39F. Wilson's Snipe. Natural size: 1¾″ long.

39G. Wilson's Phalarope. Natural size: 1⅜″ long.

39H. Wood Duck. Natural size: 3″ long.

39I. Mourning Dove. Natural size: 1¾″ long.

39J. Starling. Natural size: 2½″ long.

39K. Prairie Chicken. Natural size: 2¼″ long.

39L. Burrowing Owl. Natural size: 2¼″ long.

39M. Spotted Sandpiper. Natural size: 1¼″ long.

PLATE 40

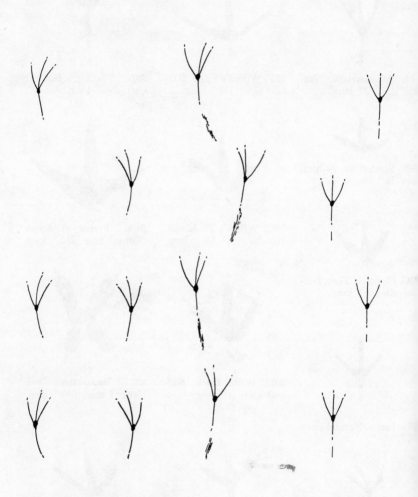

40A. Hopping and Walking Track of Robin. Natural size: 1¾" long.

40B. Walking Track of Crow. Natural size: 3" long.

40C. Walking Track of Starling. Natural size: 2½" long.

PLATE 41

41A. Walking Track of Woodcock. Natural size: 1½″ long.

41B. Walking Track of Great Blue Heron. Natural size: 8″ long.

41C. Walking Track of Mallard. Natural size: 3″ long.

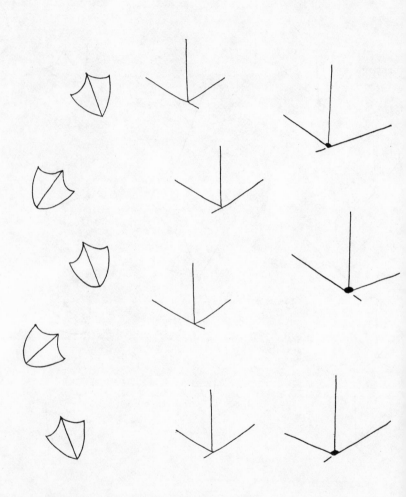

42A. Walking Track of Herring Gull. Natural size: 3½″ long.

42B. Walking Track of Wilson's Snipe in Mud. Natural size: 1¾″ long.

42C. Walking Track of Greater Yellow-legs. Natural size: 2⅛″ long.

PLATE 43

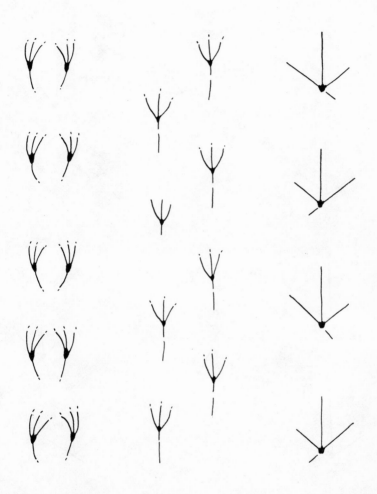

43A. Hopping Track of Sparrow. Natural size: 1⅛″ long.

43B. Walking Track of Horned Lark. Natural size: 1½″ long.

43C. Walking Track of Ring-necked Pheasant. Natural size: 3½″ long.

PLATE 44

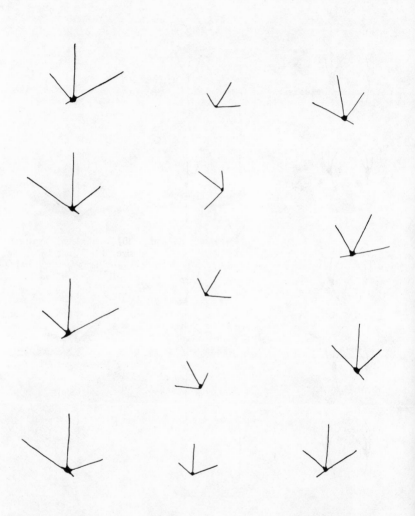

44A. Walking Track of Bobwhite. Natural size: 1½" long.

44B. Walking Track of Piping Plover. Natural size: ¾" long.

44C. Walking Track of Spotted Sandpiper. Natural size: 1¼" long.

PLATE 45   131

45A. Robin. Natural size: 1¾″ long.

45E. Horned Lark. Natural size: 1½″ long.

45I. Wood Thrush. Natural size: 2½″ long.

45B. Piping Plover. Natural size: ¾″ long.

45F. Bobwhite. Natural size: 1½″ long.

45J. Killdeer. Natural size: 1⅜″ long.

45C. Willet. Natural size: 2⅛″ long.

45G. Woodcock. Natural size: 1½″ long.

45K. Pigeon. Natural size: 2″ long.

45D. Black-necked Stilt. Natural size: 2″ long.

45H. Ruffed Grouse. Natural size: 1¾″ long.

45L. Flicker. Natural size: 1¾″ long.

46A. Walking Track of Ruffed Grouse. Natural size: 1¾" long.

46B. Running Track of Sanderling in Wet Sand. Natural size: ⅞" long.

PLATE 47   133

47A. Crow. Natural size: 3″ long.

47D. Semi - palmated Plover. Natural size: 1″ long.

47G. Mallard. Natural size: 3″ long.

47B. Sandhill Crane. Natural size: 3¾″ long.

47E. Canada Goose. Natural size: 4″ long.

47H. Coot. Natural size: 4″ long.

47C. Black - crowned Night Heron. Natural size: 4″ long.

47F. Domestic Chicken. Natural size: 4″ long.

47I. Virginia Rail. Natural size: 2⅞″ long.

48A. Prints of Bullfrog in Mud.

48C. Hopping Track of Leopard Frog in Mud.

48B. Track of Toad in Mud.

48D. Hopping Track of Spring Peeper in Mud.

PLATE 49   135

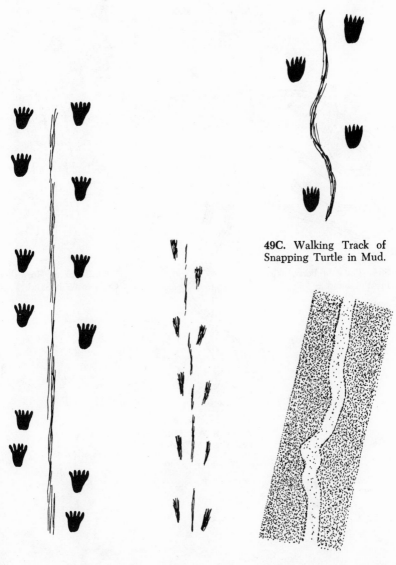

49C. Walking Track of
Snapping Turtle in Mud.

49A. Track of Painted
Turtle in Mud.

49B. Track of Lizard in
Sand.

49D. Track of Garter
Snake in Sand. Natural
size: ⅝″ wide.

50A. Track of Periwinkle in Wet Sand.

50D. Track of Horseshoe Crab in Wet Sand.

50B. Track of a Crab in Wet Sand.

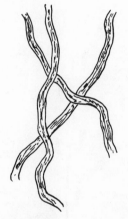

50C. Tracks of Earthworm in Wet Mud. Natural size: ¼" wide.

50E. Track of Centipede. Natural size: ⅜" wide.

PLATE 51 137

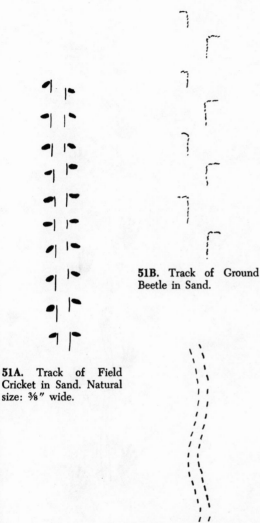

51A. Track of Field Cricket in Sand. Natural size: ⅜″ wide.

51B. Track of Ground Beetle in Sand.

51C. Track of Caterpillar (Gulf Fritillary) in Sand. Natural size: ⅛″ long, track ¼″ wide.

51D. Track of Grasshopper in Sand. Natural size: ¾″ wide.

52A. Track of Hog-nosed Snake in Sand.

52B. Walking Track of Alligator.

Index

A CATALOGUE OF
SELECTED DOVER BOOKS
IN ALL FIELDS OF INTEREST

A CATALOGUE OF SELECTED DOVER

BOOKS IN ALL FIELDS OF INTEREST

RACKHAM'S COLOR ILLUSTRATIONS FOR WAGNER'S RING. Rackham's finest mature work—all 64 full-color watercolors in a faithful and lush interpretation of the *Ring*. Full-sized plates on coated stock of the paintings used by opera companies for authentic staging of Wagner. Captions aid in following complete Ring cycle. Introduction. 64 illustrations plus vignettes. 72pp. 8⅝ x 11¼.   23779-6 Pa. $6.00

CONTEMPORARY POLISH POSTERS IN FULL COLOR, edited by Joseph Czestochowski. 46 full-color examples of brilliant school of Polish graphic design, selected from world's first museum (near Warsaw) dedicated to poster art. Posters on circuses, films, plays, concerts all show cosmopolitan influences, free imagination. Introduction. 48pp. 9⅜ x 12¼.
23780-X Pa. $6.00

GRAPHIC WORKS OF EDVARD MUNCH, Edvard Munch. 90 haunting, evocative prints by first major Expressionist artist and one of the greatest graphic artists of his time: *The Scream, Anxiety, Death Chamber, The Kiss, Madonna,* etc. Introduction by Alfred Werner. 90pp. 9 x 12.
23765-6 Pa. $5.00

THE GOLDEN AGE OF THE POSTER, Hayward and Blanche Cirker. 70 extraordinary posters in full colors, from Maitres de l'Affiche, Mucha, Lautrec, Bradley, Cheret, Beardsley, many others. Total of 78pp. 9⅜ x 12¼.   22753-7 Pa. $6.95

THE NOTEBOOKS OF LEONARDO DA VINCI, edited by J. P. Richter. Extracts from manuscripts reveal great genius; on painting, sculpture, anatomy, sciences, geography, etc. Both Italian and English. 186 ms. pages reproduced, plus 500 additional drawings, including studies for *Last Supper*, Sforza monument, etc. 860pp. 7⅞ x 10¾. (Available in U.S. only)
22572-0, 22573-9 Pa., Two-vol. set $19.90

THE CODEX NUTTALL, as first edited by Zelia Nuttall. Only inexpensive edition, in full color, of a pre-Columbian Mexican (Mixtec) book. 88 color plates show kings, gods, heroes, temples, sacrifices. New explanatory, historical introduction by Arthur G. Miller. 96pp. 11⅜ x 8½. (Available in U.S. only)   23168-2 Pa. $7.95

UNE SEMAINE DE BONTÉ, A SURREALISTIC NOVEL IN COLLAGE, Max Ernst. Masterpiece created out of 19th-century periodical illustrations, explores worlds of terror and surprise. Some consider this Ernst's greatest work. 208pp. 8⅛ x 11.   23252-2 Pa. $6.00

DRAWINGS OF WILLIAM BLAKE, William Blake. 92 plates from Book of Job, *Divine Comedy, Paradise Lost,* visionary heads, mythological figures, Laocoon, etc. Selection, introduction, commentary by Sir Geoffrey Keynes. 178pp. 8⅛ x 11. 22303-5 Pa. $5.00

ENGRAVINGS OF HOGARTH, William Hogarth. 101 of Hogarth's greatest works: *Rake's Progress, Harlot's Progress, Illustrations for Hudibras, Before and After, Beer Street and Gin Lane,* many more. Full commentary. 256pp. 11 x 13¾. 22479-1 Pa. $12.95

DAUMIER: 120 GREAT LITHOGRAPHS, Honore Daumier. Wide-ranging collection of lithographs by the greatest caricaturist of the 19th century. Concentrates on eternally popular series on lawyers, on married life, on liberated women, etc. Selection, introduction, and notes on plates by Charles F. Ramus. Total of 158pp. 9⅜ x 12¼. 23512-2 Pa. $6.00

DRAWINGS OF MUCHA, Alphonse Maria Mucha. Work reveals draftsman of highest caliber: studies for famous posters and paintings, renderings for book illustrations and ads, etc. 70 works, 9 in color; including 6 items not drawings. Introduction. List of illustrations. 72pp. 9⅜ x 12¼. (Available in U.S. only) 23672-2 Pa. $4.50

GIOVANNI BATTISTA PIRANESI: DRAWINGS IN THE PIERPONT MORGAN LIBRARY, Giovanni Battista Piranesi. For first time ever all of Morgan Library's collection, world's largest. 167 illustrations of rare Piranesi drawings—archeological, architectural, decorative and visionary. Essay, detailed list of drawings, chronology, captions. Edited by Felice Stampfle. 144pp. 9⅜ x 12¼. 23714-1 Pa. $7.50

NEW YORK ETCHINGS (1905-1949), John Sloan. All of important American artist's N.Y. life etchings. 67 works include some of his best art; also lively historical record—Greenwich Village, tenement scenes. Edited by Sloan's widow. Introduction and captions. 79pp. 8⅜ x 11¼. 23651-X Pa. $5.00

CHINESE PAINTING AND CALLIGRAPHY: A PICTORIAL SURVEY, Wan-go Weng. 69 fine examples from John M. Crawford's matchless private collection: landscapes, birds, flowers, human figures, etc., plus calligraphy. Every basic form included: hanging scrolls, handscrolls, album leaves, fans, etc. 109 illustrations. Introduction. Captions. 192pp. 8⅞ x 11¾. 23707-9 Pa. $7.95

DRAWINGS OF REMBRANDT, edited by Seymour Slive. Updated Lippmann, Hofstede de Groot edition, with definitive scholarly apparatus. All portraits, biblical sketches, landscapes, nudes, Oriental figures, classical studies, together with selection of work by followers. 550 illustrations. Total of 630pp. 9⅛ x 12¼. 21485-0, 21486-9 Pa., Two-vol. set $17.90

THE DISASTERS OF WAR, Francisco Goya. 83 etchings record horrors of Napoleonic wars in Spain and war in general. Reprint of 1st edition, plus 3 additional plates. Introduction by Philip Hofer. 97pp. 9⅜ x 8¼. 21872-4 Pa. $4.50

THE EARLY WORK OF AUBREY BEARDSLEY, Aubrey Beardsley. 157 plates, 2 in color: *Manon Lescaut, Madame Bovary, Morte Darthur, Salome,* other. Introduction by H. Marillier. 182pp. 8⅛ x 11. 21816-3 Pa. $6.50

THE LATER WORK OF AUBREY BEARDSLEY, Aubrey Beardsley. Exotic masterpieces of full maturity: *Venus and Tannhauser, Lysistrata, Rape of the Lock, Volpone,* Savoy material, etc. 174 plates, 2 in color. 186pp. 8⅛ x 11. 21817-1 Pa. $5.95

THOMAS NAST'S CHRISTMAS DRAWINGS, Thomas Nast. Almost all Christmas drawings by creator of image of Santa Claus as we know it, and one of America's foremost illustrators and political cartoonists. 66 illustrations. 3 illustrations in color on covers. 96pp. 8⅜ x 11¼.
23660-9 Pa. $3.50

THE DORÉ ILLUSTRATIONS FOR DANTE'S DIVINE COMEDY, Gustave Doré. All 135 plates from Inferno, Purgatory, Paradise; fantastic tortures, infernal landscapes, celestial wonders. Each plate with appropriate (translated) verses. 141pp. 9 x 12. 23231-X Pa. $5.00

DORÉ'S ILLUSTRATIONS FOR RABELAIS, Gustave Doré. 252 striking illustrations of *Gargantua and Pantagruel* books by foremost 19th-century illustrator. Including 60 plates, 192 delightful smaller illustrations. 153pp. 9 x 12. 23656-0 Pa. $6.00

LONDON: A PILGRIMAGE, Gustave Doré, Blanchard Jerrold. Squalor, riches, misery, beauty of mid-Victorian metropolis; 55 wonderful plates, 125 other illustrations, full social, cultural text by Jerrold. 191pp. of text. 9⅜ x 12¼. 22306-X Pa. $7.00

THE RIME OF THE ANCIENT MARINER, Gustave Doré, S. T. Coleridge. Dore's finest work, 34 plates capture moods, subtleties of poem. Full text. Introduction by Millicent Rose. 77pp. 9¼ x 12. 22305-1 Pa. $4.50

THE DORE BIBLE ILLUSTRATIONS, Gustave Doré. All wonderful, detailed plates: Adam and Eve, Flood, Babylon, Life of Jesus, etc. Brief King James text with each plate. Introduction by Millicent Rose. 241 plates. 241pp. 9 x 12. 23004-X Pa. $6.95

THE COMPLETE ENGRAVINGS, ETCHINGS AND DRYPOINTS OF ALBRECHT DURER. "Knight, Death and Devil"; "Melencolia," and more—all Dürer's known works in all three media, including 6 works formerly attributed to him. 120 plates. 235pp. 8⅜ x 11¼.
22851-7 Pa. $7.50

MECHANICK EXERCISES ON THE WHOLE ART OF PRINTING, Joseph Moxon. First complete book (1683-4) ever written about typography, a compendium of everything known about printing at the latter part of 17th century. Reprint of 2nd (1962) Oxford Univ. Press edition. 74 illustrations. Total of 550pp. 6⅛ x 9¼. 23617-X Pa. $7.95

THE COMPLETE WOODCUTS OF ALBRECHT DURER, edited by Dr. W. Kurth. 346 in all: "Old Testament," "St. Jerome," "Passion," "Life of Virgin," Apocalypse," many others. Introduction by Campbell Dodgson. 285pp. 8½ x 12¼.   21097-9 Pa. $7.50

DRAWINGS OF ALBRECHT DURER, edited by Heinrich Wolfflin. 81 plates show development from youth to full style. Many favorites; many new. Introduction by Alfred Werner. 96pp. 8⅛ x 11.   22352-3 Pa. $6.00

THE HUMAN FIGURE, Albrecht Dürer. Experiments in various techniques—stereometric, progressive proportional, and others. Also life studies that rank among finest ever done. Complete reprinting of *Dresden Sketchbook*. 170 plates. 355pp. 8⅜ x 11¼.   21042-1 Pa. $7.95

OF THE JUST SHAPING OF LETTERS, Albrecht Dürer. Renaissance artist explains design of Roman majuscules by geometry, also Gothic lower and capitals. Grolier Club edition. 43pp. 7⅞ x 10¾   21306-4 Pa. $3.00

TEN BOOKS ON ARCHITECTURE, Vitruvius. The most important book ever written on architecture. Early Roman aesthetics, technology, classical orders, site selection, all other aspects. Stands behind everything since. Morgan translation. 331pp. 5⅜ x 8½.   20645-9 Pa. $5.00

THE FOUR BOOKS OF ARCHITECTURE, Andrea Palladio. 16th-century classic responsible for Palladian movement and style. Covers classical architectural remains, Renaissance revivals, classical orders, etc. 1738 Ware English edition. Introduction by A. Placzek. 216 plates. 110pp. of text. 9½ x 12¾.   21308-0 Pa. $10.00

HORIZONS, Norman Bel Geddes. Great industrialist stage designer, "father of streamlining," on application of aesthetics to transportation, amusement, architecture, etc. 1932 prophetic account; function, theory, specific projects. 222 illustrations. 312pp. 7⅞ x 10¾.   23514-9 Pa. $6.95

FRANK LLOYD WRIGHT'S FALLINGWATER, Donald Hoffmann. Full, illustrated story of conception and building of Wright's masterwork at Bear Run, Pa. 100 photographs of site, construction, and details of completed structure. 112pp. 9¼ x 10.   23671-4 Pa. $5.95

THE ELEMENTS OF DRAWING, John Ruskin. Timeless classic by great Viltorian; starts with basic ideas, works through more difficult. Many practical exercises. 48 illustrations. Introduction by Lawrence Campbell. 228pp. 5⅜ x 8½.   22730-8 Pa. $3.75

GIST OF ART, John Sloan. Greatest modern American teacher, Art Students League, offers innumerable hints, instructions, guided comments to help you in painting. Not a formal course. 46 illustrations. Introduction by Helen Sloan. 200pp. 5⅜ x 8½.   23435-5 Pa. $4.00

THE ANATOMY OF THE HORSE, George Stubbs. Often considered the great masterpiece of animal anatomy. Full reproduction of 1766 edition, plus prospectus; original text and modernized text. 36 plates. Introduction by Eleanor Garvey. 121pp. 11 x 14¾.   23402-9 Pa. $8.95

BRIDGMAN'S LIFE DRAWING, George B. Bridgman. More than 500 illustrative drawings and text teach you to abstract the body into its major masses, use light and shade, proportion; as well as specific areas of anatomy, of which Bridgman is master. 192pp. 6½ x 9¼. (Available in U.S. only)
                                                                22710-3 Pa. $4.50

ART NOUVEAU DESIGNS IN COLOR, Alphonse Mucha, Maurice Verneuil, Georges Auriol. Full-color reproduction of *Combinaisons ornementales* (c. 1900) by Art Nouveau masters. Floral, animal, geometric, interlacings, swashes—borders, frames, spots—all incredibly beautiful. 60 plates, hundreds of designs. 9⅜ x 8-1/16.   22885-1 Pa. $4.50

FULL-COLOR FLORAL DESIGNS IN THE ART NOUVEAU STYLE, E. A. Seguy. 166 motifs, on 40 plates, from *Les fleurs et leurs applications decoratives* (1902): borders, circular designs, repeats, allovers, "spots." All in authentic Art Nouveau colors. 48pp. 9⅜ x 12¼.
                                                                23439-8 Pa. $5.00

A DIDEROT PICTORIAL ENCYCLOPEDIA OF TRADES AND IN-DUSTRY, edited by Charles C. Gillispie. 485 most interesting plates from the great French Encyclopedia of the 18th century show hundreds of working figures, artifacts, process, land and cityscapes; glassmaking, paper-making, metal extraction, construction, weaving, making furniture, clothing, wigs, dozens of other activities. Plates fully explained. 920pp. 9 x 12.
                                22284-5, 22285-3 Clothbd., Two-vol. set $40.00

HANDBOOK OF EARLY ADVERTISING ART, Clarence P. Hornung. Largest collection of copyright-free early and antique advertising art ever compiled. Over 6,000 illustrations, from Franklin's time to the 1890's for special effects, novelty. Valuable source, almost inexhaustible.
Pictorial Volume. Agriculture, the zodiac, animals, autos, birds, Christmas, fire engines, flowers, trees, musical instruments, ships, games and sports, much more. Arranged by subject matter and use. 237 plates. 288pp. 9 x 12.
                                                                20122-8 Clothbd. $15.00

Typographical Volume. Roman and Gothic faces ranging from 10 point to 300 point, "Barnum," German and Old English faces, script, logotypes, scrolls and flourishes, 1115 ornamental initials, 67 complete alphabets, more. 310 plates. 320pp. 9 x 12.   20123-6 Clothbd. $15.00

CALLIGRAPHY (CALLIGRAPHIA LATINA), J. G. Schwandner. High point of 18th-century ornamental calligraphy. Very ornate initials, scrolls, borders, cherubs, birds, lettered examples. 172pp. 9 x 13.
                                                                20475-8 Pa. $7.95

ART FORMS IN NATURE, Ernst Haeckel. Multitude of strangely beautiful natural forms: Radiolaria, Foraminifera, jellyfishes, fungi, turtles, bats, etc. All 100 plates of the 19th-century evolutionist's *Kunstformen der Natur* (1904). 100pp. 9⅜ x 12¼. 22987-4 Pa. $5.00

CHILDREN: A PICTORIAL ARCHIVE FROM NINETEENTH-CENTURY SOURCES, edited by Carol Belanger Grafton. 242 rare, copyright-free wood engravings for artists and designers. Widest such selection available. All illustrations in line. 119pp. 8⅜ x 11¼.
23694-3 Pa. $4.00

WOMEN: A PICTORIAL ARCHIVE FROM NINETEENTH-CENTURY SOURCES, edited by Jim Harter. 391 copyright-free wood engravings for artists and designers selected from rare periodicals. Most extensive such collection available. All illustrations in line. 128pp. 9 x 12.
23703-6 Pa. $4.95

ARABIC ART IN COLOR, Prisse d'Avennes. From the greatest ornamentalists of all time—50 plates in color, rarely seen outside the Near East, rich in suggestion and stimulus. Includes 4 plates on covers. 46pp. 9⅜ x 12¼. 23658-7 Pa. $6.00

AUTHENTIC ALGERIAN CARPET DESIGNS AND MOTIFS, edited by June Beveridge. Algerian carpets are world famous. Dozens of geometrical motifs are charted on grids, color-coded, for weavers, needleworkers, craftsmen, designers. 53 illustrations plus 4 in color. 48pp. 8¼ x 11. (Available in U.S. only) 23650-1 Pa. $1.75

DICTIONARY OF AMERICAN PORTRAITS, edited by Hayward and Blanche Cirker. 4000 important Americans, earliest times to 1905, mostly in clear line. Politicians, writers, soldiers, scientists, inventors, industrialists, Indians, Blacks, women, outlaws, etc. Identificatory information. 756pp. 9¼ x 12¾. 21823-6 Clothbd. $65.00

HOW THE OTHER HALF LIVES, Jacob A. Riis. Journalistic record of filth, degradation, upward drive in New York immigrant slums, shops, around 1900. New edition includes 100 original Riis photos, monuments of early photography. 233pp. 10 x 7⅞. 22012-5 Pa. $7.00

NEW YORK IN THE THIRTIES, Berenice Abbott. Noted photographer's fascinating study of city shows new buildings that have become famous and old sights that have disappeared forever. Insightful commentary. 97 photographs. 97pp. 11⅜ x 10. 22967-X Pa. $6.00

MEN AT WORK, Lewis W. Hine. Famous photographic studies of construction workers, railroad men, factory workers and coal miners. New supplement of 18 photos on Empire State building construction. New introduction by Jonathan L. Doherty. Total of 69 photos. 63pp. 8 x 10¾.
23475-4 Pa. $4.00

CATALOGUE OF DOVER BOOKS

THE DEPRESSION YEARS AS PHOTOGRAPHED BY ARTHUR ROTH-STEIN, Arthur Rothstein. First collection devoted entirely to the work of outstanding 1930s photographer: famous dust storm photo, ragged children, unemployed, etc. 120 photographs. Captions. 119pp. 9¼ x 10¾.
23590-4 Pa. **$5.95**

CAMERA WORK: A PICTORIAL GUIDE, Alfred Stieglitz. All 559 illustrations and plates from the most important periodical in the history of art photography, Camera Work (1903-17). Presented four to a page, reduced in size but still clear, in strict chronological order, with complete captions. Three indexes. Glossary. Bibliography. 176pp. 8⅜ x 11¼.
23591-2 Pa. $6.95

ALVIN LANGDON COBURN, PHOTOGRAPHER, Alvin L. Coburn. Revealing autobiography by one of greatest photographers of 20th century gives insider's version of Photo-Secession, plus comments on his own work. 77 photographs by Coburn. Edited by Helmut and Alison Gernsheim. 160pp. 8⅛ x 11.-
23685-4 Pa. $6.00

NEW YORK IN THE FORTIES, Andreas Feininger. 162 brilliant photographs by the well-known photographer, formerly with Life magazine, show commuters, shoppers, Times Square at night, Harlem nightclub, Lower East Side, etc. Introduction and full captions by John von Hartz. 181pp. 9¼ x 10¾.
23585-8 Pa. $6.95

GREAT NEWS PHOTOS AND THE STORIES BEHIND THEM, John Faber. Dramatic volume of 140 great news photos, 1855 through 1976, and revealing stories behind them, with both historical and technical information. Hindenburg disaster, shooting of Oswald, nomination of Jimmy Carter, etc. 160pp. 8¼ x 11.
23667-6 Pa. **$6.00**

THE ART OF THE CINEMATOGRAPHER, Leonard Maltin. Survey of American cinematography history and anecdotal interviews with 5 masters—Arthur Miller, Hal Mohr, Hal Rosson, Lucien Ballard, and Conrad Hall. Very large selection of behind-the-scenes production photos. 105 photographs. Filmographies. Index. Originally Behind the Camera. 144pp. 8¼ x 11.
23686-2 Pa. $5.00

DESIGNS FOR THE THREE-CORNERED HAT (LE TRICORNE), Pablo Picasso. 32 fabulously rare drawings—including 31 color illustrations of costumes and accessories—for 1919 production of famous ballet. Edited by Parmenia Migel, who has written new introduction. 48pp. 9⅜ x 12¼. (Available in U.S. only)
23709-5 Pa. $5.00

NOTES OF A FILM DIRECTOR, Sergei Eisenstein. Greatest Russian filmmaker explains montage, making of Alexander Nevsky, aesthetics; comments on self, associates, great rivals (Chaplin), similar material. 78 illustrations. 240pp. 5⅜ x 8½.
22392-2 Pa. $7.00

HOLLYWOOD GLAMOUR PORTRAITS, edited by John Kobal. 145 photos capture the stars from 1926-49, the high point in portrait photography. Gable, Harlow, Bogart, Bacall, Hedy Lamarr, Marlene Dietrich, Robert Montgomery, Marlon Brando, Veronica Lake; 94 stars in all. Full background on photographers, technical aspects, much more. Total of 160pp. 8⅜ x 11¼. 23352-9 Pa. $6.95

THE NEW YORK STAGE: FAMOUS PRODUCTIONS IN PHOTO-GRAPHS, edited by Stanley Appelbaum. 148 photographs from Museum of City of New York show 142 plays, 1883-1939. *Peter Pan, The Front Page, Dead End, Our Town,* O'Neill, hundreds of actors and actresses, etc. Full indexes. 154pp. 9½ x 10. 23241-7 Pa. $6.00

DIALOGUES CONCERNING TWO NEW SCIENCES, Galileo Galilei. Encompassing 30 years of experiment and thought, these dialogues deal with geometric demonstrations of fracture of solid bodies, cohesion, leverage, speed of light and sound, pendulums, falling bodies, accelerated motion, etc. 300pp. 5⅜ x 8½. 60099-8 Pa. $5.50

THE GREAT OPERA STARS IN HISTORIC PHOTOGRAPHS, edited by James Camner. 343 portraits from the 1850s to the 1940s: Tamburini, Mario, Caliapin, Jeritza, Melchior, Melba, Patti, Pinza, Schipa, Caruso, Farrar, Steber, Gobbi, and many more—270 performers in all. Index. 199pp. 8⅜ x 11¼. 23575-0 Pa. $7.50

J. S. BACH, Albert Schweitzer. Great full-length study of Bach, life, background to music, music, by foremost modern scholar. Ernest Newman translation. 650 musical examples. Total of 928pp. 5⅜ x 8½. (Available in U.S. only) 21631-4, 21632-2 Pa., Two-vol. set $12.00

COMPLETE PIANO SONATAS, Ludwig van Beethoven. All sonatas in the fine Schenker edition, with fingering, analytical material. One of best modern editions. Total of 615pp. 9 x 12. (Available in U.S. only) 23134-8, 23135-6 Pa., Two-vol. set $17.90

KEYBOARD MUSIC, J. S. Bach. Bach-Gesellschaft edition. For harpsichord, piano, other keyboard instruments. English Suites, French Suites, Six Partitas, Goldberg Variations, Two-Part Inventions, Three-Part Sinfonias. 312pp. 8⅛ x 11. (Available in U.S. only) 22360-4 Pa. $7.95

FOUR SYMPHONIES IN FULL SCORE, Franz Schubert. Schubert's four most popular symphonies: No. 4 in C Minor ("Tragic"); No. 5 in B-flat Major; No. 8 in B Minor ("Unfinished"); No. 9 in C Major ("Great"). Breitkopf & Hartel edition. Study score. 261pp. 9⅜ x 12¼. 23681-1 Pa. $8.95

THE AUTHENTIC GILBERT & SULLIVAN SONGBOOK, W. S. Gilbert, A. S. Sullivan. Largest selection available; 92 songs, uncut, original keys, in piano rendering approved by Sullivan. Favorites and lesser-known fine numbers. Edited with plot synopses by James Spero. 3 illustrations. 399pp. 9 x 12. 23482-7 Pa. $10.95

PRINCIPLES OF ORCHESTRATION, Nikolay Rimsky-Korsakov. Great classical orchestrator provides fundamentals of tonal resonance, progression of parts, voice and orchestra, tutti effects, much else in major document. 330pp. of musical excerpts. 489pp. 6½ x 9¼. 21266-1 Pa. $7.50

TRISTAN UND ISOLDE, Richard Wagner. Full orchestral score with complete instrumentation. Do not confuse with piano reduction. Commentary by Felix Mottl, great Wagnerian conductor and scholar. Study score. 655pp. 8⅛ x 11. 22915-7 Pa. $13.95

REQUIEM IN FULL SCORE, Giuseppe Verdi. Immensely popular with choral groups and music lovers. Republication of edition published by C. F. Peters, Leipzig, n. d. German frontmaker in English translation. Glossary. Text in Latin. Study score. 204pp. 9⅜ x 12¼.
23682-X Pa. $6.50

COMPLETE CHAMBER MUSIC FOR STRINGS, Felix Mendelssohn. All of Mendelssohn's chamber music: Octet, 2 Quintets, 6 Quartets, and Four Pieces for String Quartet. (Nothing with piano is included). Complete works edition (1874-7). Study score. 283 pp. 9⅜ x 12¼.
23679-X Pa. $7.50

POPULAR SONGS OF NINETEENTH-CENTURY AMERICA, edited by Richard Jackson. 64 most important songs: "Old Oaken Bucket," "Arkansas Traveler," "Yellow Rose of Texas," etc. Authentic original sheet music, full introduction and commentaries. 290pp. 9 x 12. 23270-0 Pa. $7.95

COLLECTED PIANO WORKS, Scott Joplin. Edited by Vera Brodsky Lawrence. Practically all of Joplin's piano works—rags, two-steps, marches, waltzes, etc., 51 works in all. Extensive introduction by Rudi Blesh. Total of 345pp. 9 x 12. 23106-2 Pa. $15.95

BASIC PRINCIPLES OF CLASSICAL BALLET, Agrippina Vaganova. Great Russian theoretician, teacher explains methods for teaching classical ballet; incorporates best from French, Italian, Russian schools. 118 illustrations. 175pp. 5⅜ x 8½. 22036-2 Pa. $2.75

CHINESE CHARACTERS, L. Wieger. Rich analysis of 2300 characters according to traditional systems into primitives. Historical-semantic analysis to phonetics (Classical Mandarin) and radicals. 820pp. 6⅛ x 9¼.
21321-8 Pa. $12.50

THE WARES OF THE MING DYNASTY, R. L. Hobson. Foremost scholar examines and illustrates many varieties of Ming (1368-1644). Famous blue and white, polychrome, lesser-known styles and shapes. 117 illustrations, 9 full color, of outstanding pieces. Total of 263pp. 6⅛ x 9¼. (Available in U.S. only) 23652-8 Pa. $6.00

AN ETYMOLOGICAL DICTIONARY OF MODERN ENGLISH, Ernest Weekley. Richest, fullest work, by foremost British lexicographer. Detailed word histories. Inexhaustible. Do not confuse this with *Concise Etymological Dictionary*, which is abridged. Total of 856pp. 6½ x 9¼.
21873-2, 21874-0 Pa., Two-vol. set $13.00

A MAYA GRAMMAR, Alfred M. Tozzer. Practical, useful English-language grammar by the Harvard anthropologist who was one of the three greatest American scholars in the area of Maya culture. Phonetics, grammatical processes, syntax, more. 301pp. 5⅜ x 8½. 23465-7 Pa. $4.00

THE JOURNAL OF HENRY D. THOREAU, edited by Bradford Torrey, F. H. Allen. Complete reprinting of 14 volumes, 1837-61, over two million words; the sourcebooks for *Walden*, etc. Definitive. All original sketches, plus 75 photographs. Introduction by Walter Harding. Total of 1804pp. 8½ x 12¼. 20312-3, 20313-1 Clothbd., Two-vol. set $80.00

CLASSIC GHOST STORIES, Charles Dickens and others. 18 wonderful stories you've wanted to reread: "The Monkey's Paw," "The House and the Brain," "The Upper Berth," "The Signalman," "Dracula's Guest," "The Tapestried Chamber," etc. Dickens, Scott, Mary Shelley, Stoker, etc. 330pp. 5⅜ x 8½. 20735-8 Pa. $4.50

SEVEN SCIENCE FICTION NOVELS, H. G. Wells. Full novels. *First Men in the Moon, Island of Dr. Moreau, War of the Worlds, Food of the Gods, Invisible Man, Time Machine, In the Days of the Comet.* A basic science-fiction library. 1015pp. 5⅜ x 8½. (Available in U.S. only) 20264-X Clothbd. $15.00

ARMADALE, Wilkie Collins. Third great mystery novel by the author of *The Woman in White* and *The Moonstone*. Ingeniously plotted narrative shows an exceptional command of character, incident and mood. Original magazine version with 40 illustrations. 597pp. 5⅜ x 8½. 23429-0 Pa. $7.95

FLATLAND, E. A. Abbott. Science-fiction classic explores life of 2-D being in 3-D world. Read also as introduction to thought about hyperspace. Introduction by Banesh Hoffmann. 16 illustrations. 103pp. 5⅜ x 8½. 20001-9 Pa. $2.75

AYESHA: THE RETURN OF "SHE," H. Rider Haggard. Virtuoso sequel featuring the great mythic creation, Ayesha, in an adventure that is fully as good as the first book, *She*. Original magazine version, with 47 original illustrations by Maurice Greiffenhagen. 189pp. 6½ x 9¼. 23649-8 Pa. $3.50

ORIENTAL RUGS, ANTIQUE AND MODERN, Walter A. Hawley. Persia, Turkey, Caucasus, Central Asia, China, other traditions. Best general survey of all aspects: styles and periods, manufacture, uses, symbols and their interpretation, and identification. 96 illustrations, 11 in color. 320pp. 6⅛ x 9¼. 22366-3 Pa. $6.95

CHINESE POTTERY AND PORCELAIN, R. L. Hobson. Detailed descriptions and analyses by former Keeper of the Department of Oriental Antiquities and Ethnography at the British Museum. Covers hundreds of pieces from primitive times to 1915. Still the standard text for most periods. 136 plates, 40 in full color. Total of 750pp. 5⅜ x 8½. 23253-0 Pa. $10.00

UNCLE SILAS, J. Sheridan LeFanu. Victorian Gothic mystery novel, considered by many best of period, even better than Collins or Dickens. Wonderful psychological terror. Introduction by Frederick Shroyer. 436pp. 5⅜ x 8½. 21715-9 Pa. **$6.95**

JURGEN, James Branch Cabell. The great erotic fantasy of the 1920's that delighted thousands, shocked thousands more. Full final text, Lane edition with 13 plates by Frank Pape. 346pp. 5⅜ x 8½.
23507-6 Pa. $4.50

THE CLAVERINGS, Anthony Trollope. Major novel, chronicling aspects of British Victorian society, personalities. Reprint of Cornhill serialization, 16 plates by M. Edwards; first reprint of full text. Introduction by Norman Donaldson. 412pp. 5⅜ x 8½. 23464-9 Pa. $5.00

KEPT IN THE DARK, Anthony Trollope. Unusual short novel about Victorian morality and abnormal psychology by the great English author. Probably the first American publication. Frontispiece by Sir John Millais. 92pp. 6½ x 9¼. 23609-9 Pa. $2.50

RALPH THE HEIR, Anthony Trollope. Forgotten tale of illegitimacy, inheritance. Master novel of Trollope's later years. Victorian country estates, clubs, Parliament, fox hunting, world of fully realized characters. Reprint of 1871 edition. 12 illustrations by F. A. Faser. 434pp. of text. 5⅜ x 8½. 23642-0 Pa. $6.50

YEKL and THE IMPORTED BRIDEGROOM AND OTHER STORIES OF THE NEW YORK GHETTO, Abraham Cahan. Film *Hester Street* based on *Yekl* (1896). Novel, other stories among first about Jewish immigrants of N.Y.'s East Side. Highly praised by W. D. Howells—Cahan "a new star of realism." New introduction by Bernard G. Richards. 240pp. 5⅜ x 8½. 22427-9 Pa. $3.50

THE HIGH PLACE, James Branch Cabell. Great fantasy writer's enchanting comedy of disenchantment set in 18th-century France. Considered by some critics to be even better than his famous *Jurgen*. 10 illustrations and numerous vignettes by noted fantasy artist Frank C. Pape. 320pp. 5⅜ x 8½. 23670-6 Pa. $4.00

ALICE'S ADVENTURES UNDER GROUND, Lewis Carroll. Facsimile of ms. Carroll gave Alice Liddell in 1864. Different in many ways from final Alice. Handlettered, illustrated by Carroll. Introduction by Martin Gardner. 128pp. 5⅜ x 8½. 21482-6 Pa. $2.50

FAVORITE ANDREW LANG FAIRY TALE BOOKS IN MANY COLORS, Andrew Lang. The four Lang favorites in a boxed set—the complete *Red, Green, Yellow* and *Blue* Fairy Books. 164 stories; 439 illustrations by Lancelot Speed, Henry Ford and G. P. Jacomb Hood. Total of about 1500pp. 5⅜ x 8½. 23407-X Boxed set, Pa. $16.95

HOUSEHOLD STORIES BY THE BROTHERS GRIMM. All the great Grimm stories: "Rumpelstiltskin," "Snow White," "Hansel and Gretel," etc., with 114 illustrations by Walter Crane. 269pp. 5⅜ x 8½.
21080-4 Pa. $3.50

SLEEPING BEAUTY, illustrated by Arthur Rackham. Perhaps the fullest, most delightful version ever, told by C. S. Evans. Rackham's best work. 49 illustrations. 110pp. 7⅞ x 10¾. 22756-1 Pa. $2.95

AMERICAN FAIRY TALES, L. Frank Baum. Young cowboy lassoes Father Time; dummy in Mr. Floman's department store window comes to life; and 10 other fairy tales. 41 illustrations by N. P. Hall, Harry Kennedy, Ike Morgan, and Ralph Gardner. 209pp. 5⅜ x 8½. 23643-9 Pa. $3.00

THE WONDERFUL WIZARD OF OZ, L. Frank Baum. Facsimile in full color of America's finest children's classic. Introduction by Martin Gardner. 143 illustrations by W. W. Denslow. 267pp. 5⅜ x 8½.
20691-2 Pa. $4.50

THE TALE OF PETER RABBIT, Beatrix Potter. The inimitable Peter's terrifying adventure in Mr. McGregor's garden, with all 27 wonderful, full-color Potter illustrations. 55pp. 4¼ x 5½. (Available in U.S. only)
22827-4 Pa. $1.50

THE STORY OF KING ARTHUR AND HIS KNIGHTS, Howard Pyle. Finest children's version of life of King Arthur. 48 illustrations by Pyle. 131pp. 6⅛ x 9¼. 21445-1 Pa. $5.95

CARUSO'S CARICATURES, Enrico Caruso. Great tenor's remarkable caricatures of self, fellow musicians, composers, others. Toscanini, Puccini, Farrar, etc. Impish, cutting, insightful. 473 illustrations. Preface by M. Sisca. 217pp. 8⅜ x 11¼. 23528-9 Pa. $6.95

PERSONAL NARRATIVE OF A PILGRIMAGE TO ALMADINAH AND MECCAH, Richard Burton. Great travel classic by remarkably colorful personality. Burton, disguised as a Moroccan, visited sacred shrines of Islam, narrowly escaping death. Wonderful observations of Islamic life, customs, personalities. 47 illustrations. Total of 959pp. 5⅜ x 8½.
21217-3, 21218-1 Pa., Two-vol. set $14.00

INCIDENTS OF TRAVEL IN YUCATAN, John L. Stephens. Classic (1843) exploration of jungles of Yucatan, looking for evidences of Maya civilization. Travel adventures, Mexican and Indian culture, etc. Total of 669pp. 5⅜ x 8½. 20926-1, 20927-X Pa., Two-vol. set $7.90

AMERICAN LITERARY AUTOGRAPHS FROM WASHINGTON IRVING TO HENRY JAMES, Herbert Cahoon, et al. Letters, poems, manuscripts of Hawthorne, Thoreau, Twain, Alcott, Whitman, 67 other prominent American authors. Reproductions, full transcripts and commentary. Plus checklist of all American Literary Autographs in The Pierpont Morgan Library. Printed on exceptionally high-quality paper. 136 illustrations. 212pp. 9⅛ x 12¼. 23548-3 Pa. $12.50

CATALOGUE OF DOVER BOOKS

AN AUTOBIOGRAPHY, Margaret Sanger. Exciting personal account of hard-fought battle for woman's right to birth control, against prejudice, church, law. Foremost feminist document. 504pp. 5⅜ x 8½.
20470-7 Pa. $7.50

MY BONDAGE AND MY FREEDOM, Frederick Douglass. Born as a slave, Douglass became outspoken force in antislavery movement. The best of Douglass's autobiographies. Graphic description of slave life. Introduction by P. Foner. 464pp. 5⅜ x 8½.
22457-0 Pa. $6.50

LIVING MY LIFE, Emma Goldman. Candid, no holds barred account by foremost American anarchist: her own life, anarchist movement, famous contemporaries, ideas and their impact. Struggles and confrontations in America, plus deportation to U.S.S.R. Shocking inside account of persecution of anarchists under Lenin. 13 plates. Total of 944pp. 5⅜ x 8½.
22543-7, 22544-5 Pa., Two-vol. set $12.00

LETTERS AND NOTES ON THE MANNERS, CUSTOMS AND CONDITIONS OF THE NORTH AMERICAN INDIANS, George Catlin. Classic account of life among Plains Indians: ceremonies, hunt, warfare, etc. Dover edition reproduces for first time all original paintings. 312 plates. 572pp. of text. 6⅛ x 9¼.
22118-0, 22119-9 Pa.. Two-vol. set $12.00

THE MAYA AND THEIR NEIGHBORS, edited by Clarence L. Hay, others. Synoptic view of Maya civilization in broadest sense, together with Northern, Southern neighbors. Integrates much background, valuable detail not elsewhere. Prepared by greatest scholars: Kroeber, Morley, Thompson, Spinden, Vaillant, many others. Sometimes called Tozzer Memorial Volume. 60 illustrations, linguistic map. 634pp. 5⅜ x 8½.
23510-6 Pa. $10.00

HANDBOOK OF THE INDIANS OF CALIFORNIA, A. L. Kroeber. Foremost American anthropologist offers complete ethnographic study of each group. Monumental classic. 459 illustrations, maps. 995pp. 5⅜ x 8½.
23368-5 Pa. $13.00

SHAKTI AND SHAKTA, Arthur Avalon. First book to give clear, cohesive analysis of Shakta doctrine, Shakta ritual and Kundalini Shakti (yoga). Important work by one of world's foremost students of Shaktic and Tantric thought. 732pp. 5⅜ x 8½. (Available in U.S. only)
23645-5 Pa. $7.95

AN INTRODUCTION TO THE STUDY OF THE MAYA HIEROGLYPHS, Syvanus Griswold Morley. Classic study by one of the truly great figures in hieroglyph research. Still the best introduction for the student for reading Maya hieroglyphs. New introduction by J. Eric S. Thompson. 117 illustrations. 284pp. 5⅜ x 8½.
23108-9 Pa. $4.00

A STUDY OF MAYA ART, Herbert J. Spinden. Landmark classic interprets Maya symbolism, estimates styles, covers ceramics, architecture, murals, stone carvings as artforms. Still a basic book in area. New introduction by J. Eric Thompson. Over 750 illustrations. 341pp. 8⅜ x 11¼.
21235-1 Pa. $6.95

GEOMETRY, RELATIVITY AND THE FOURTH DIMENSION, Rudolf Rucker. Exposition of fourth dimension, means of visualization, concepts of relativity as Flatland characters continue adventures. Popular, easily followed yet accurate, profound. 141 illustrations. 133pp. 5⅜ x 8½.
23400-2 Pa. $2.75

THE ORIGIN OF LIFE, A. I. Oparin. Modern classic in biochemistry, the first rigorous examination of possible evolution of life from nitrocarbon compounds. Non-technical, easily followed. Total of 295pp. 5⅜ x 8½.
60213-3 Pa. $5.95

PLANETS, STARS AND GALAXIES, A. E. Fanning. Comprehensive introductory survey: the sun, solar system, stars, galaxies, universe, cosmology; quasars, radio stars, etc. 24pp. of photographs. 189pp. 5⅜ x 8½. (Available in U.S. only)
21680-2 Pa. $3.75

THE THIRTEEN BOOKS OF EUCLID'S ELEMENTS, translated with introduction and commentary by Sir Thomas L. Heath. Definitive edition. Textual and linguistic notes, mathematical analysis, 2500 years of critical commentary. Do not confuse with abridged school editions. Total of 1414pp. 5⅜ x 8½.
60088-2, 60089-0, 60090-4 Pa., Three-vol. set $19.50